Stage Lighting

STEP-BY-STEP

Stage Lighting

STEP-BY-STEP

Basic techniques
to achieve professional results

Graham Walters

A & C Black • London

A QUARTO BOOK

First published 1997
A & C Black (Publishers) Limited
35 Bedford Row
London WCIR 4JH

ISBN 0-7136-4639-X

A CIP catalogue record for
this book is available from the British
Library

Designed and produced by
Quarto Publishing plc
The Old Brewery
6 Blundell Street
London N7 9BH

Senior editor Michelle Pickering
Senior art editor Elizabeth Healey
Designer Tanya Devonshire-Jones
Copy editor Sandy Ransford
Illustrators Yanos Marffy,
Stuart Robertson, Gary Cross
and Dave Kemp
Photographer Paul Forrester
Picture researcher Zoe Holtermann
Art director Moira Clinch
Assistant art director Penny Cobb
Editorial director Pippa Rubenstein

Typeset by Central Southern
Typesetters, Eastbourne, UK
Manufactured by Universal Graphics
(Pte) Ltd, Singapore
Printed by Leefung-Asco
Printers Ltd, China

Contents

Creating Special Effects

Production

Introduction

In writing this book I hope to provide an uncomplicated, informative and interesting guide to how to light stage productions. I have deliberately written it from the standpoint of a complete novice who knows little about the theatre and who is curious to find out what it might all be about. There is no assumption that you, the reader and potential lighting designer, have even been inside a theatre, or that you have any knowledge of electricity. In other words, this is exactly the kind of book I wished I had had when I took over my first theatre.

This book aims to provide you with a broad introduction to theatrical lighting. Note that I said introduction. If you think that after reading this book you will be able to light a production of *La Traviata* at La Scala, Milan, you must think again! As with any other art, it takes time to become accomplished, for experience of your medium is one of the most valuable skills any artist can acquire. However, after reading this book, you will be able to approach lighting most small- to medium-scale productions with reasonable confidence, which will increase as your experience grows.

To become a professional lighting designer, you should attend a course, and there are many excellent ones. These can range from an evening class at a local college to a full-time degree course at university. They will provide you with experience, knowledge and confidence, as well as a professional qualification should you so desire. One of the other advantages of taking a course is that you will have access to lighting equipment and a theatre space which you may not have otherwise. Another good way to gain access to lighting equipment is to join an amateur theatrical group which may have the use of school premises, for example, so that you can get a chance to learn by experience. Use any such opportunities well – experience is the best teacher.

When I referred to stage lighting as an art, it was not a slip. Lighting is as much a part of the artistic process as any other aspect of work in the theatre. The lighting designer helps to tell the story, by illuminating the text and creating the emotional world of colour and light that brings the production to life. Lighting designers rarely get the kind of public adulation that actors or directors do, but they are no less artists for all that, and they play a vital role in the staging of a theatrical production.

Although at the beginning the whole thing may appear to be impossibly complicated and technical, don't panic! This book is intended to reduce the lighting process to a series of tasty, bite-sized chunks, easily consumed and digested. You will have to bend your brain around a few simple formulae, remember a few names and understand a few principles. But it isn't that difficult. The thing to remember is that theatre is magic, and lighting for theatre is part of that magic. I have always loved theatre, particularly the process of creating a wonderful, moving experience from just an idea – it's fantastic! And I hope you will come to enjoy the process too, if you are not already involved. So it's "beginners on stage" and "curtain-up". Here we go, and "break a leg!"

Graham Walters

THE ART OF STAGE LIGHTING

Light is not just something we turn on and off at a switch or shine on to things; it is what and how we see. Some of the ancient Greeks thought we see things because our eyes send out rays which bounce off things in our environment and are received back into the eye, rather as an echo works with sound. Of course, this theory doesn't work at night, and the Greeks' explanation for this was that our eyes get tired as the day progresses and so cannot give out as many rays. It took several hundred years for anyone else to come up with a credible theory of how we see and what light is. But now we know that the visible world is a world of light, provided by the sun, and reflected and refracted by our environment to be received and interpreted by the light-sensitive receptors in our eyes to create the world we see around us.

If we think of the ways in which light affects us, we can see how it can be shaped and manipulated to influence an audience. Think of torchlight processions and the use that was made of them by the Nazis. Things seem much more profound and primal by the light of a naked flame. Candlelight can be very romantic; the shadows cast by a candle flame can be terrifying. A stream of bright morning sunshine through a window can make one feel full of optimism; the same window filled with moonlight can be

Stage lighting can produce magical results, enhancing the colours and movements of the performing artist to stunning effect.

mysterious. So why not just use natural light for productions?

Well you can, of course, and sometimes you may have to. But it is not controllable, and it fixes the production in time and space, and restricts the performance times to the hours of daylight. The use of lighting can change the time frame of the production in an instant. You can use it to enhance the emotional content of the piece, to create an atmosphere, to help sculpt the set, to intensify the costume design. Stage lighting helps to heighten the unique experience of being swept away for a couple of hours in a theatre.

Anyone thinking of becoming a shaper of light should start by coming to understand how light and colour affect them. Look around your own environment and start to see the world around you in terms of colour, light and shade. See how light makes the world into three dimensions by adding modelling and depth. Look at how a painter uses a knowledge of this to create the illusion of three dimensions on a flat surface. Remember, the lighting designer is a visual artist; you must paint with light, tell stories with it, and make us feel happy, or sad, or experience someone else's pain.

A BRIEF HISTORY OF STAGE LIGHTING

Along with so many aspects of technology, stage lighting has changed rapidly over the last hundred years, and the change has accelerated in recent years. The advent of computer-controlled lighting has affected the art at every level. Comparing a modern, flexible rig with one of 20 years ago is like staring back into the dim and distant past. So what were things like before that? Even before electricity? The answers are fascinating. For it seems that as long as humankind has taken time out to perform, we have been at pains to improve the art and show it off to its greatest advantage. Even when theatre in its more ritualized form was performed in the open during ancient times,

torchlight or the natural effects of light were taken into consideration. Many ancient rituals still take place at night by firelight, as they must have done for thousands of years.

Most performers would have shared the same conditions as the audience. Mystery plays, for example, were generally performed outdoors on movable stages which would rumble from street to street to entertain people. The performers of the *commedia dell'arte*, which evolved from the ancient Roman theatre, would set up a trestle stage in a market place and play there, sharing the elements with the people they came to entertain. There is, however, ample evidence that the Greeks and Romans used both natural

and artificial light to enhance performances. In one ancient Greek amphitheatre, for example, I noticed it had been positioned so the sun set directly behind the acting area. The Greeks often used large sheets of polished mica to reflect the sun's rays on to the acting area to "lift" it, and to highlight the actors.

It was not until the 16th century that any significant developments took place. The Italian theatre had benefited from the flowering of the Renaissance, and was becoming increasingly complex. They had also begun to move theatre indoors, which allowed a greater division between the audience and the performers, and they began to develop the conventions of the theatre as we know them today.

This engraving shows the open-air theatre of Dionysius in Athens. The ancient Greeks often built their theatres so that the sun would shine onto the acting area throughout the day and set behind the stage at night.

For example, they discovered that tragedy was better played in darker conditions and comedy in brighter light, and that the appearance of the stage area could be highlighted by darkening the auditorium.

Around this time the combination of lighting and scenery was developed. Even if a single light source were used, the scenery could be painted to give the impression that the light came from a different direction, so adding reality to the scene. They also performed experiments in colouring light, by placing candles or oil lamps behind flasks of coloured water.

The 17th century witnessed an explosion of the theatrical arts, along with the upsurge in European culture at that time.

Painters became experts in the representation of light. Paintings of the period not only display a keen sense of colour and light, but also a sense of theatre and presentation of events.

The masque, a stage spectacular which mixed all the stage arts in an extravagant fashion, became popular at this time. Some of the accounts of the staging of these events are extraordinary. They make a modern rock concert sound tame in comparison. And all of the lighting was accomplished by candles and oil lamps. Because of the great upsurge of interest in new theatrical techniques, and hence the developments in lighting, most productions could move indoors and be played at night. People began to use footlights, and even devised methods of dimming the lights.

In the 18th century people developed greater control over lighting in theatres. They introduced reflectors to direct the

light, coloured silks to colour it, and a greater co-ordination between stage design and lighting began. The design of the oil lamp and wick were improved, and, along with the introduction of the coloured glass chimney, allowed even greater flexibility.

The arrival of gas lighting in the 1820s heralded a revolution in stage lighting. It was followed closely by the introduction of limelight and the carbon arc, and developments continued throughout the century. As gas became more widely available and gas burners improved, greater effects could be created. Soon a full dim to black was possible, and the first spotlight was invented. The arrival of electric light began the series of huge technical developments in lighting that have occurred in the 20th century. The advent of the cinema, and of film lighting, have also served to accelerate both the art and technology of this medium.

In this woodcut of a 15th-century Italian theatre, the seating area is covered but the stage is still open to the sunlight.

Nowadays, most theatres are indoors, allowing greater control of the stage lighting. Here, footlights help to emphasize the threatening, almost primeval atmosphere of the scene.

Making a Start

For many people their only experience of theatre is as a paying member of the audience. You will have bought your ticket, had a drink at the bar, queued to find your seat, settled in as the house lights dimmed, and watched the play presented to you by the acting company. You may have enjoyed it or hated it, and finally left the building. You will have done all of this without necessarily understanding the processes that occur during, before and after the show, or of the world that exists outside of the area the audience inhabits. Like any other business, theatre has a variety of conventions, jobs and jargon, which are largely unknown outside of the theatrical world. So let us take a quick journey through this world to see how a theatre functions, what its various parts are called, what happens in them and what they do. Once you have some idea of the shape of a theatre and how it runs we will begin to explore the world of lighting. We will start at the beginning with some basic theories of electricity and then look at each stage in the process of creating a lighting design that will help to bring a production to life.

The Empty Space

A theatre can be anywhere. Any space in which a performance takes place is a theatre. In recent years one London theatre company offered to perform a condensed version of *Psycho* in your bathroom. Others would take audiences on to underground trains and create a performance among the passengers. All a theatre needs are performers, an audience and a space for both to be in. It is then up to the creators of the piece of theatre to decide how to use, transform and inhabit that space. Many companies around the world create site-specific performances or events, which may be performed anywhere from a derelict building to Sydney Harbour Bridge. As a lighting designer you are liable to encounter many different spaces to light, from a conventional theatre space to a gym or an upstairs room. If you are to be concerned with conventional theatre, however, with four walls, a front, a back and a roof, it is wise as well as useful to have a working knowledge of how the building is structured, the location of its parts and what each is called.

1	Front of house
2	Box office
3	Public bar
4	Public toilets
5	Admin
6	Lighting box
7	Auditorium
8	Stage
9	Trap doors
10	Prompt corner
11	Scene dock
12	Dock doors
13	Green room
14	Stage door
15	Dressing rooms
16	Wardrobe
17	Light store
18	Rehearsal room

THEATRE LAYOUT
Most theatres have the same basic structures, although they are not always in the same places. This can become confusing. Here, however, is a rough guide to where everything is and what it is called. It is a good idea to become familiar with these terms, if you are not already, not only for your own good but for the confidence of the team you work with.

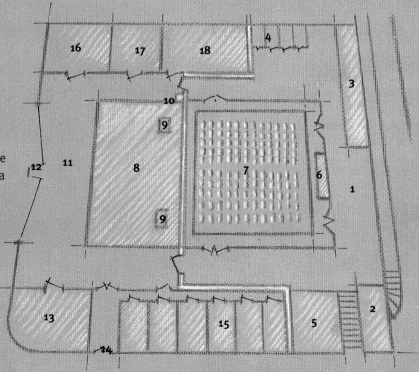

FRONT OF HOUSE

This is the area which lies in front of the stage. It includes the auditorium, the foyer, the bar, the ticket office and the toilets (for customers).

BOX OFFICE

Most theatres have a box office in the front foyer to sell and dispense pre-paid tickets to the public.

AUDITORIUM

The auditorium is the room in which the audience sits to watch or listen to the performance.

ORCHESTRA (STALLS)

In larger theatres which have more than one level of seating in the auditorium, the lowest level of seating, on the floor of the auditorium, is called the orchestra or stalls.

BACKSTAGE

Backstage is the area of a theatre which lies behind the performing area. It contains all the facilities which serve the production on stage: the dressing-rooms, the wardrobe, the stage mechanics, plus all the personnel who take part in productions.

STAGE DOOR

This is the entrance from the street into the backstage area, and hence to the stage.

DRESSING ROOMS

Situated backstage, these are the rooms (or sometimes room!) in which the performers dress and get made-up for their parts.

GREEN ROOM

This is a communal room or area backstage where all staff can meet together to relax, eat meals or entertain guests.

WARDROBE

This can be one room or a whole department. Situated backstage, it is the place where the costumes are made, maintained and often also stored.

WINGS

These are the hidden bits at the side of a stage or performing area where the actors wait to go on stage. Stage management and an assortment of technicians and anxious producers may also be found here.

FLIES

This is the area above the stage in which scenery, lighting and other equipment is hung out of sight, or "flown", hence the name.

PROMPT CORNER

This is a desk and console at the side of the stage from which the stage manager runs the show.

LIGHTING BOX

This is the room from which the technicians run the show. It contains the lighting control board, sound controls, and so on. It is generally situated at the back of the auditorium, with a view over the heads of the audience. A glass panel separates the crew from the public and allows them to see the production they are lighting.

SCENE DOCK

In this store room you may find scenery, flats, cycloramas and all the other paraphernalia which may be used to dress the stage. It is generally found backstage.

DOCK DOORS

These are the doors through which you load all the production paraphernalia into the theatre. In many theatres they take you into the scene store; in others they lead on to the stage.

LIGHT STORE

This is generally a room situated backstage, on stage, sometimes under the stage, or even under the audience seating-blocks, in which the lanterns, gel clamps and so on are stored.

ADMIN

The administration offices are where the people who deal with the day-to-day running of the theatre work, for example the administrator and finance officer.

STUDIO

If the theatre is large enough, it may have a studio attached to it. This is used as a small-scale theatre venue and allows for touring productions and lower budget works to be staged.

REHEARSAL ROOM

Generally speaking, most theatres do not have a rehearsal room, at least not on the premises. Rehearsals are generally conducted in rented spaces due to space constraints.

Theatre Shapes

You should now have some idea of the parts that make up a theatre, though you can never be quite sure of what you will find. Even in conventional theatres, the shape and style of the performing areas can vary greatly. In many, the space is mutable and can be re-arranged in a number of different forms. These different styles of performing space fall into a number of broad categories.

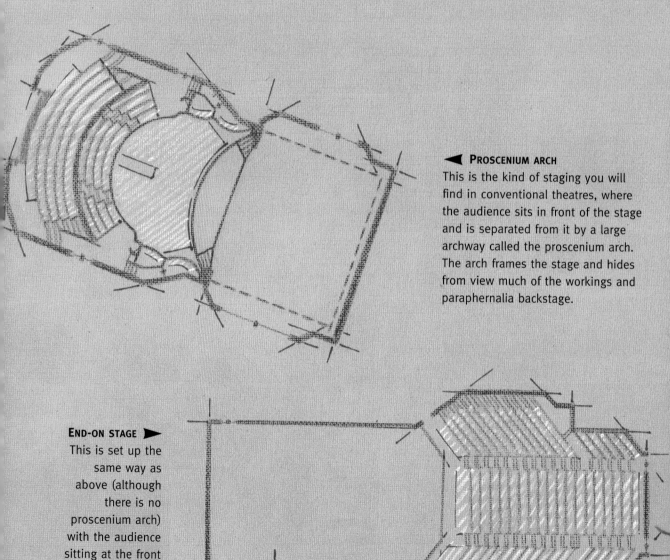

◀ **PROSCENIUM ARCH**
This is the kind of staging you will find in conventional theatres, where the audience sits in front of the stage and is separated from it by a large archway called the proscenium arch. The arch frames the stage and hides from view much of the workings and paraphernalia backstage.

END-ON STAGE ▶
This is set up the same way as above (although there is no proscenium arch) with the audience sitting at the front of the stage.

THRUST STAGE

A thrust stage literally thrusts out into the auditorium and has an audience sitting on three sides of it.

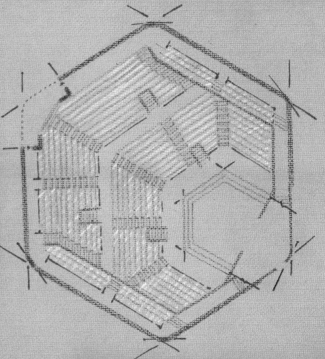

A thrust stage (above) takes the show out into the audience, allowing them to see into the acting area.

A theatre with changeable space (above) allows acting companies to change the layout of the stage and seating areas to suit their needs.

▲ CHANGEABLE SPACE

More and more theatre spaces are now mutable, which means that the audience seating-blocks can be moved to create any of the other staging permutations described here. The seating can be dispensed with altogether, and the action of the play then takes place among the audience, moving from place to place around the auditorium.

IN THE ROUND

Here the performing area is surrounded by the audience. There may be a stage or just an arena.

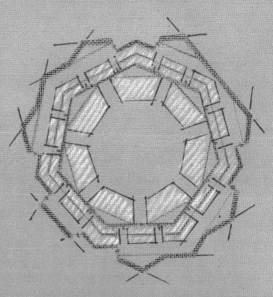

Who Does What and Where

A theatre, like any other place of work, needs specialized staff to make it run. Each job and position in the theatre has its name and recognized function. However, depending on the size of the company, some of the positions may be combined. In the smallest companies they may be combined into two or even one position! As a lighting designer you will have to deal with some or all of these people, so you should have some idea of how the whole business is likely to be arranged.

Artistic director

ARTISTIC DIRECTOR

At the top of any organization in the theatre, whether building-based or a touring company, is the artistic director. He or she not only has responsibility for the overall running of the building or company, but also has to give it its artistic identity. The artistic director directs much of the company's work as well as commissioning pieces and deciding which productions to bring into the house. They also preside over the hiring and firing of theatre personnel.

Administrator

ADMINISTRATOR

Nowadays the artistic director is just above, or, more frequently, shares the top slot with the theatre administrator, who looks after the administrative side of running the company. Apart from day-to-day issues, and generally seeing that the company functions, he or she has overall responsibility for the budget – a considerable task. It also falls to him or her to do the support work for productions.

Production manager

PRODUCTION MANAGER

There is a very close relationship between both of the aforementioned posts and that of the production manager. He or she is in charge of the running of every production put on by the theatre or created by the company. The need to manage the budget necessitates close co-operation with the administrator, as well as ensuring that the wishes of the artistic director are carried out.

Head of lighting

DEPARTMENTAL HEADS

Alongside the production manager are the heads of the various departments. In larger theatres these are permanent posts, although sometimes they may be combined. Smaller-scale companies may hire people to fill these posts for the duration of a particular production. The departments concerned are lighting and sound, and costume and set. The musical director and choreographer may also be temporary posts.

Electricians

ELECTRICIANS

Next comes the chief electrician, often with an assistant electrician, and then the crew, with whom you will be working closely. They are responsible for the servicing and upkeep of all electrical equipment, and also help to rig and focus the lighting.

Stage crew

STAGE CREW

Working with the electrical staff are the stage manager, deputy stage manager, assistant stage manager and the rest of the stage crew. They have overall responsibility for the running of rehearsals and performances. They hire rehearsal space, buy props and look after actors, ensuring that they arrive on stage at the right time and with the right prop, and much, much more. They are usually wonderfully capable and resourceful people for whom no task seems too difficult, and their talents mean the difference between chaos and success. The stage management crew also does all the shifting and moving, flying and flooding that the production requires on stage.

Wardrobe staff

WARDROBE STAFF

There will also be a wardrobe supervisor, wardrobe assistants and dressers, who look after the costumes. They may make them, repair them, and wash, clean and press them, either for the next performance or for storage. The dressers costume the actors each night of the performance.

Props department

PROPS DEPARTMENT

Larger houses retain a head of props and assistants to look after them, maintain and build props for productions, and a master carpenter plus assistants for scenery- and furniture-making.

Performing artists

PERFORMING ARTISTS

Last but not least, and somewhat at a distance from this set-up, comes the performing company, who are primarily concerned with the artistic director, musical director, choreographer, etc.

Basic Electrical Theory and Safety

It is essential that anyone who is going to be using lighting should have a sound knowledge of things electrical. This does not mean a masters degree in electrical engineering, but it does mean that you should know what you are dealing with and how it works. Electricity can kill, so treat it with respect.

WHAT IS ELECTRICITY?

Electricity, for our purposes, consists of the flow of particles – called electrons – which exist in everything around us, including ourselves. In fact, our own nervous system works on electrical impulses.

An electrical circuit can be likened to a water-pumping system. A pump, which exerts pressure on the water, forces water through the pipes of the water system between two points. Likewise, electrons are forced between two points through an electrical circuit by a generator or battery. What causes the flow in each case is a difference in pressure between the two points. This pressure exerted on the flow of electrons is measured in volts, and the difference in pressure in an electric circuit is called a difference in potential.

Now, the greater the amount of pressure exerted on the flow of water, the greater the quantity of water that will pass through the system in a given time. The same is true of electricity. This flow of electrons is called the current and is measured in amps. The flow of water will also be affected by the width of the pipes. The wider the pipe, the more water that can flow through it. Electricity is similarly affected by the material through which it is flowing. Different materials offer differing amounts of resistance to this flow. The resistance of a substance is measured in ohms. There are two broad categories of materials: conductors and insulators. Conductors have a low resistance to electricity and allow it to pass with ease; insulators impede the flow, sometimes to the point of stopping it altogether.

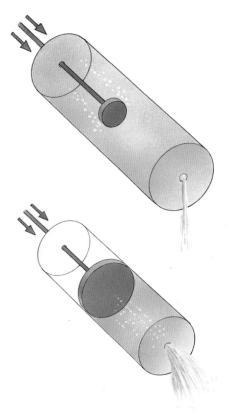

Using the analogy of a water-pumping system, if you increase the amount of pressure exerted on the water, more will flow through the pipes. The same is true of electricity.

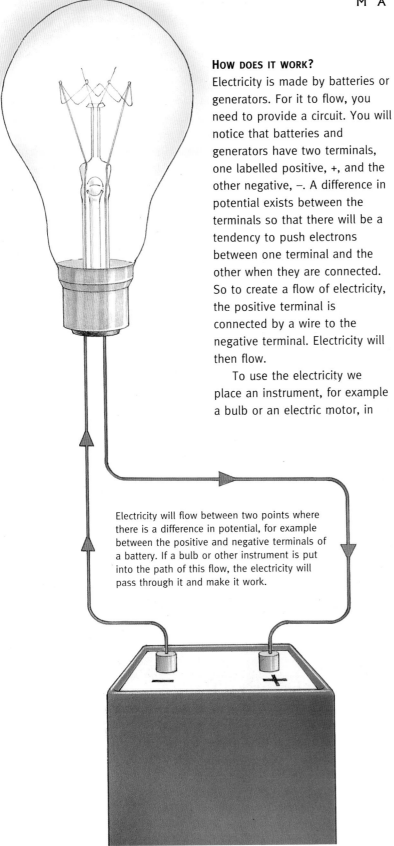

HOW DOES IT WORK?

Electricity is made by batteries or generators. For it to flow, you need to provide a circuit. You will notice that batteries and generators have two terminals, one labelled positive, +, and the other negative, –. A difference in potential exists between the terminals so that there will be a tendency to push electrons between one terminal and the other when they are connected. So to create a flow of electricity, the positive terminal is connected by a wire to the negative terminal. Electricity will then flow.

To use the electricity we place an instrument, for example a bulb or an electric motor, in the circuit. The electricity will then flow through the bulb or motor and make it work. With domestic electricity, the flow originates at the power station. This travels through a conductor (the live wire) to wherever it is needed and then returns via another conductor (the neutral wire) to its source. Again, this is driven by the pressure or potential difference and is measured in volts.

Electricity will flow between two points where there is a difference in potential, for example between the positive and negative terminals of a battery. If a bulb or other instrument is put into the path of this flow, the electricity will pass through it and make it work.

HOW IS IT CONTROLLED?

There are only two ways to regulate the energy in an electrical circuit. One is to regulate the voltage of the source. This is not always possible, however, as with the mains supply – each country in the world has a standard voltage for its mains power supply. In this case, a resistance must be introduced into the circuit. If the resistance is made variable, then the energy or the current can be slowed or reduced by varying amounts. This can all be calculated by using the formula:

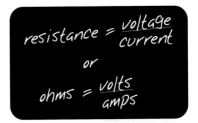

$$resistance = \frac{voltage}{current}$$
$$or$$
$$ohms = \frac{volts}{amps}$$

Therefore, if you only need a certain amount of current to flow through a circuit that is supplied from the fixed voltage of the mains, you can work out how much resistance to put into the circuit to produce that current.

WHAT IS A WATT?

Let us just re-cap on that. Voltage is the pressure applied to the flow of electrons. Amps refers to the amount of electron flow, or the current. Resistance to this flow is measured in ohms.

The other measurement to be taken into account when dealing with things electrical is how much power is required by an individual instrument to make it work. This has to be known so that the instrument, motor, bulb, etc, will work properly. Not enough power and it will work slowly or be dim or not work at all. The wattage is the amount of power used by an electrical device. This is worked out using the following formula:

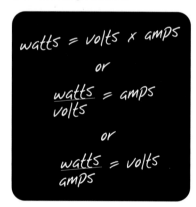

$$watts = volts \times amps$$
$$or$$
$$\frac{watts}{volts} = amps$$
$$or$$
$$\frac{watts}{amps} = volts$$

ALTERNATING CURRENT

So far we have been considering current which travels in one direction. This is called direct current. However, the domestic electricity supplied to us comes in the form of alternating current. This is a flow of electricity which, after reaching a maximum in one direction, decreases and finally reverses until it reaches a maximum in the opposite direction when it reverses once more. This process is called a cycle and is repeated constantly. The number of such cycles per second is called the frequency and is measured in hertz. Each country has its own frequency.

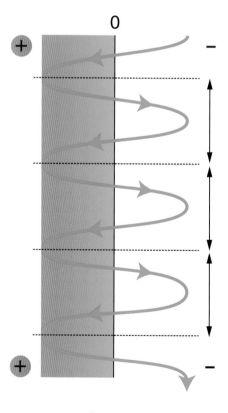

THE MAINS SUPPLY

Electricity is normally distributed from the power station in three separate supplies called phases. When the three phases or supplies arrive at a building they are separated by the mains distribution board. Normally each phase is treated as a separate supply and is routed to a different part of the building. If these different phases come into contact with each other, the voltages may combine to produce an amount which could prove lethal. In theatre lighting terms, all phases go to a dimmer room and are distributed from there. It is worth repeating that the three phases must not be connected to each other either by cable, metalwork or any other kind of conductor. The theatre's lighting plan should clearly show the distribution of the phases and each socket outlet should be colour coded to show which phase powers it.

Alternating current consists of electrons flowing back and forth between the positive and negative terminals. Each section of the diagram represents a single cycle.

EARTHING

Cables are used to deliver electricity from the dimmer room to wherever it is needed and then return the flow to the system. Each of these cables contains a live (flow) conductor and a neutral (return) conductor. It also contains a third conductor called the earth conductor, protective conductor or simply the earth.

Electricity can escape to earth (by which I mean the planet Earth, the ground, the big round thing beneath your feet!) at any time it is flowing through a circuit. For example, if you were to touch a live conductor, the electricity would flow through your body to the earth, as the earth has a zero potential. This would give you an electric shock. If the voltage is high enough, it will kill you.

Everything metallic in your home's wiring system should be connected to earth via the earth conductor, which will be found as one of the wires in the circuit cables. So if any piece of equipment in the circuit malfunctions, the electricity will escape to earth through the earth conductor and so prevent the voltage on any exposed metal surface from rising very much higher than earth voltage. Hence, it will not be dangerous.

The length of wire inside the fuse becomes part of the circuit. It will melt if too much current passes through, thus breaking the circuit so that the excessive power cannot reach and damage the equipment.

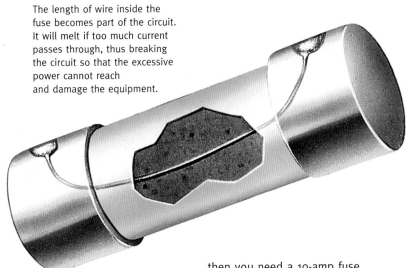

FUSES

The other protection built into all wiring systems is the fuse, with which most people are familiar. This is a short length of wire conductor designed to melt if too high a current passes through it, thus protecting the rest of the circuit from damage. This can occur if you try to use too many appliances on one circuit, for example. However, an increase in current can also occur if a fault on an appliance lowers its resistance, such as a short circuit or if electricity is leaking to earth.

Every live wire or conductor in a circuit must be protected against excess current by a fuse. The current at which the fuse melts is known as its rating, and the rating of a fuse in an electrical installation should not exceed the lowest rated conductor in the circuit. So if your cables are rated at 10 amps, then you need a 10-amp fuse between the cable and the supply. As the live side of a circuit is potentially the most dangerous – in other words, it is the one that can give you a shock or start a fire – the fuse must be inserted here. Remember that you must always replace a fuse with one of equal voltage and current rating.

Most plug outlets are standardized, for example a household 13-amp socket. If you have one such plug outlet to run your lanterns from, using the aforementioned formula you will have 240 volts x 13 amps = 3120 watts. So the power you have to run your lanterns is 3120 watts. This means that you could run six 500-watt lanterns, which at full intensity would consume 3000 watts of power. If you added another lantern, this would overload the system and cause the fuse to blow.

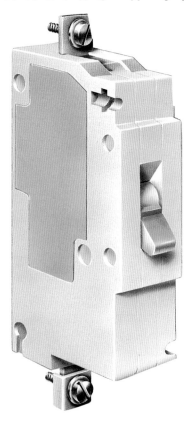

CIRCUIT BREAKERS

In most theatres the plugs have a higher amerage than that of the regular domestic plugs, and they don't usually have fuses. Instead there is a circuit breaker, which performs the same function as a fuse, that is, it prevents an overload of the system and the consequent loud bang. It is a current-sensitive switch which automatically cuts the circuit if there is a current overload. Remember to find out what the fault is, rectify it and only then switch the circuit back on!

SERIES AND PARALLEL WIRING

If a number of appliances are connected in series, then the total current passes through each of the appliances in the circuit. Normally, if you connect an appliance into a circuit, the voltage must match that of the supply. Two appliances connected in series will share the voltage of the supply, dividing it in half. So by using series wiring, it becomes possible to run a number of low-voltage bulbs, for example, from a higher voltage supply. To find out how many bulbs can be run in series from a supply, simply divide the voltage of the bulb into the voltage rating of the supply. This is how some Christmas tree lights work.

A parallel wiring system divides the total current between several appliances connected across the system, but the voltage of each appliance has to be equal to that of the supply. Most domestic appliances are connected in this way. With series wiring, if one appliance malfunctions, then the rest of the system is likely to go down, unlike with parallel wiring.

The circuit breaker shown above has a simple switch. If it is in the "on" position, electricity can flow through; if there is a surge of electricity, it will flip to "off", thus breaking the flow.

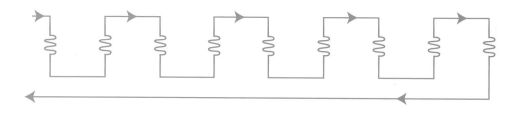

With series wiring (above), the current passes through each appliance in turn. If there is a problem with one of the appliances, the current cannot complete the circuit and therefore none of the appliances will work. Nowadays, resistors can be built in to solve this problem.

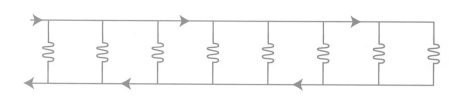

With parallel wiring (above), if there is a problem with one of the appliances, the current can simply bypass it and complete its circuit so that the others will still work.

CABLES

In most theatres, a lighting rig will change from production to production. This means that any lighting design will be of a temporary nature. To allow for this, cables must be used to carry the power to the lanterns so that they can be positioned in the desired places. Because cables have to be moved around such a lot, they are usually flexible. They should be of an approved safety design and must also be of the correct gauge to carry the required current. Flexibility is accomplished by twining groups of thin strands of conductor wire into one strand. This is then protected by an insulating coat. Solid wire is sometimes used, but only for permanent installations.

Cables generally consist of three cores or smaller cables bound together in a protective sheath. Each wire in a cable will be colour coded and performs a different function. The colours inform you of which wire should be connected to which terminal on any plug or appliance. The standard colours are as follows:

live	neutral	earth
red	black or blue	green
brown		green & yellow

Some cables will have only two wires instead of three; these wires will be live and neutral.

All standard cables have a current limit and this must be taken into account when planning the lighting of a show. If they are overloaded with current, they may burn out and blow a fuse or cause a fire. It also affects the number of lanterns which can be run. To check that a particular lantern will not overload the cable and blow a fuse, or worse still cause a fire, we go back to the formula:

$$watts = \frac{amps}{volts}$$

so if you wished to power a 1000-watt lantern from a 240-volt supply:

$$\frac{1000}{240} = 4.2 \ amps$$

So your cable would have to be able to carry 4.2 amps of current safely. The capacity of each dimmer rack must also be taken into overall calculation. But more of that later.

A three-core cable (right) is the most common type. The three wires are live, neutral and earth.

A multi-core cable (left) allows you to run lots of wires to a single place neatly. It may contain wires in many different colours, but the live, earth and neutral wires will always follow the standard colour coding.

A two-core cable (left) consists of a live and neutral wire only.

Beginning the Process

You have probably seen old films, usually black and white musicals, in which people decide to "put on a show". They set to work and, miraculously, in a matter of minutes, the script has been written, the costumes made, the set built and all the numbers choreographed. The whole show (probably including the lighting) has been conjured out of nothing through the magic of theatre and presented, complete and perfect, to the rapturous audience who turn up on the off-chance a show might be opening that night. I am constantly amazed that this view of the processes involved in theatre is held by so many people outside the profession. If only it were true, and all we had to do was say: "Hey, kids, let's put on a show, and let's do it right here!" And scenes of people engaged in short, frenetic bursts of activity would culminate in a magnificently successful opening night shortly afterwards. Well, it ain't like that, folks. Making theatre is a long and skilled process, which is as interesting and creative as the performance of the end product itself. It gives you a fantastic feeling to start with just an idea and end up with a production you are proud of, creating something wonderful from nothing. Let us now look at how this process begins, and then grows towards the final goal of the finished production.

Notes for Friday's rehearsal
Find out where chorus stands; is he always in the same place? should he be integrated into the scenes?
Need to hire: extra gels; another follow spot; talk to Richard to confirm venue has dry-ice machine.
Talk to Sarah about camp fires; practicals or hidden lanterns?

STUDYING THE SCRIPT

The starting point must be, of course, the piece to be performed – the script, the dance, the opera score, and so on. You must know the story, the characters and the setting of the piece you are going to light. What is the mood of the piece? What is the style to be? What world do you wish to create, and what do you want the audience to feel? You have to reach agreement with your team, forming a collective vision of mood and style in which the elements will not conflict but will complement each other.

You must consider the historical and geographical setting of the piece, its design, the shape of the set or sets, the colour of the costumes and the style of make-up. Next comes the venue. It is no use creating a wonderful lighting design if the place in which you are playing is the wrong shape, or hasn't enough lanterns or power. If the show is to tour, you must also take into account the kind of venues it will tour to. You may have to take lanterns with you. The budget is especially important. You must know how much you can spend on effects and stage staff to determine how many lanterns you can use and how much power you will have at your disposal.

MUSTERING YOUR RESOURCES

The first resource is the equipment. You must find out from the venue or venues how many lanterns they have, of what power and what type, and how many can be run from the lighting system. Do they have a good supply of gels and gel holders or will you have to supply your own? Next you will need to know if the budget will allow you to hire extra lanterns or effects.

The staffing must be considered. How many people will be available to rig the lights? This is important as it will affect the amount of time you will need to set up. It may be possible for the venue to pre-rig for you, so all you have to do is send them the lighting design and then go in and make fine adjustments.

DECIDING ON YOUR NEEDS

After you have read the script you should have an inkling of the task ahead. You will have to try to plan how to use your time most efficiently. You must have some idea of how many rehearsals you should attend, and at what stages of the production you should be there.

You should also be thinking of the technical rehearsal and how long you will need to ensure that your design is working properly. As we shall discuss later, time, especially time on stage, becomes very precious towards the end of the production period. So it is good to stake your claim early on so that the other people involved work around your schedule. Tensions run high as opening night approaches.

COLOURS, EFFECTS AND PRACTICALS

The lighting designer should begin working on these as soon as possible. You will get some idea of what kinds of effects you might need from the script, and colours and practicals, such as desk lamps or neon signs, will be suggested by the set and costume designs. As I mentioned above, what you can get in this department will depend on the venue and the budget. Be prepared to change your mind or have it changed by the director as the production progresses.

THE PRODUCTION SCHEDULE

As well as budget and resources, the amount of time available to produce a show is of vital importance. The period of time over which a production is crafted is called the production period, and it incorporates the whole process from design to marketing and rehearsals, and of course the lighting.

Production schedules vary from company to company, play to play and country to country. You may find yourself having to produce a finished show in a matter of weeks or a matter of months. There are no hard and fast rules, and the length of the production period can vary according to budget or established practice. However, for the purposes of this book, let us say that the production period is twelve weeks from preparation to opening night. This can be divided into three main phases:

1. Preparation: from 12 weeks to seven weeks before the opening.
2. Development: from six weeks to seven days before the opening.
3. Production week: the seven days up to the opening.

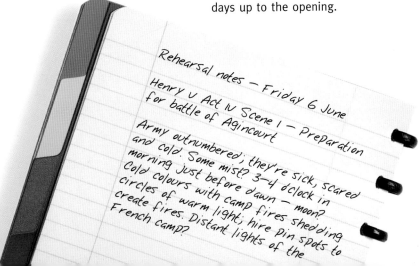

Rehearsal notes — Friday 6 June
Henry V Act IV Scene 1 — Preparation for battle of Agincourt
Army outnumbered; they're sick, scared and cold. Some mist? 3–4 o'clock in morning just before dawn — moon?
Cold colours with camp fires shedding circles of warm light; hire pin spots to create fires. Distant lights of the French camp?

Dividing the Stage

Every performance space is divided into a number of areas which conform to a world-wide convention. This makes sense when you think about it, as it saves the director giving stage directions like: "Walk down there on the left ... no, your left not mine ... and stop by that curtain thing. Yes, the one with the rip ... and say your lines, then step back ... No! Back, not sideways!" And so on – although some directors do give stage directions like this! In an effort to avoid confusion, a system has evolved over the years, and the lighting designer has to be familiar with it in order to understand the shape of the production and how to light it.

Stages can be divided into nine main areas:
ur upstage right; **uc** upstage centre;
ul upstage left; **cr** centre stage right; **c** centre
stage; **cl** centre stage left; **dr** downstage right;
dc downstage centre; **dl** downstage left.

STAGE LEFT AND STAGE RIGHT
These are the sides of the stage from the point of view of a person standing on the stage and looking out at the audience. In other words, stage left for the actor is on the right for the audience. For a thrust stage, the areas are designated with reference to the front of the acting area. For theatre in the round, they are often decided in an arbitrary fashion, for example based on the location of the main entrance.

UPSTAGE AND DOWNSTAGE
Upstage is the general direction of the back of the acting area away from the audience; downstage is towards the front of the acting area, towards the

audience. Although two actors may be in the downstage area, one may be said to be upstage of the other, that is, slightly behind him. Likewise, if you are in front of someone on the stage, that is, nearer to the audience than they are, you are said to be downstage of them.

CENTRE STAGE

Centre stage is the area at the centre of the stage, halfway between the front and the back, and the right and the left.

COMBINING THE ELEMENTS

Now that we have names for the back and front of the stage, its left, right and middle, we can combine them to divide the acting space into nine areas: downstage right, downstage centre, downstage left; centre right, centre stage, centre left; upstage right, upstage centre, upstage left.

PROMPT SIDE AND OPPOSITE PROMPT SIDE

The prompt side is the side of the stage where the stage manager usually sits with the script. From here he or she calls the actors on to the stage, announces the acts and scenes, and if needs be prompts an actor who has dried and forgotten his or her lines. Convention has it that this is usually on the stage left side, although it often isn't. But tradition persists and stage left is called prompt side. Stage right is known as opposite prompt or OP.

THE WINGS

The wings are on either side of the acting area and are usually shielded from the audience. They conceal the actors who are ready to go on, scenery waiting to be changed, stage management, stage hands and so on. With a thrust stage or theatre in the round, the wing space is often absent or minimal.

THE FLIES

This is the area above the stage where scenery and lighting equipment can be hung out of sight of the audience.

PROSCENIUM ARCH

This is the archway that frames the stage in traditional theatres, separating the actors from the audience and forming the "fourth wall".

TABS

These are curtains hung from the flies, usually the house curtain which is drawn across the proscenium arch, though it can also refer to smaller side curtains used to shield the wings.

THE GRID SYSTEM

The lighting designer must have an accurate plan of the stage, broken down into easy reference areas, to enable him or her to light it correctly. It is possible to use the conventions already described, but this can become cumbersome and may break down if the areas to be lit extend beyond the conventional ones

designated. The conventional system is rather general, and if the actor is not to disappear into the gloom, the lighting designer needs a more accurate system of dividing up the stage.

The simplest way to do it is to use a grid system. The precise division depends on the size of the stage, the shape of the set, and the number of lanterns you have to cover the area. It is probably best to base it on the conventional nine sections, treating each as a stage in its own right. Each should have its own 45-degree front lighting, and maybe, if you have the resources, its own back, side and even down lighting, to ensure that each area of the stage is evenly and properly lit. These areas should be clearly labelled on the plan, so that each lantern can be rigged and focused on the appropriate spot, and as long as the actors stick to the grid blocks, the lighting designer will be able to predict where they will be at any moment in the play and have the appropriate illumination on them.

Just how you label your grid is up to you, but probably the least confusing way is to label one side with letters and the other with numbers, that is the X axis A, B, C, D, etc, and the Y axis 1, 2, 3, 4, etc. This method is easy to remember and use, and it also allows the accommodation and labelling of additional areas, should they require lighting.

Planning

You must work from a basis of knowledge right from the beginning, so that the lighting plan grows out of the initial planning stage rather than being superimposed on it at a later date. For example, you need to know the shape and height of the set as soon as possible. There is nothing worse than trying to rig your precious lighting design only to find that half your beautifully wrought effects are obscured by bits of the set or the theatre. Not only is this deeply annoying, it can also be time consuming, and is the last thing you want in a tight schedule. Sometimes you must allow for the fact that set designers build bits on to the set that have never been mentioned in a meeting or seen on a plan. But the more planning you can do in advance, the easier your task will be.

As well as studying the script, a lighting designer should gather together as much material from other departments as possible to get a clear idea of the look and mood of the play.

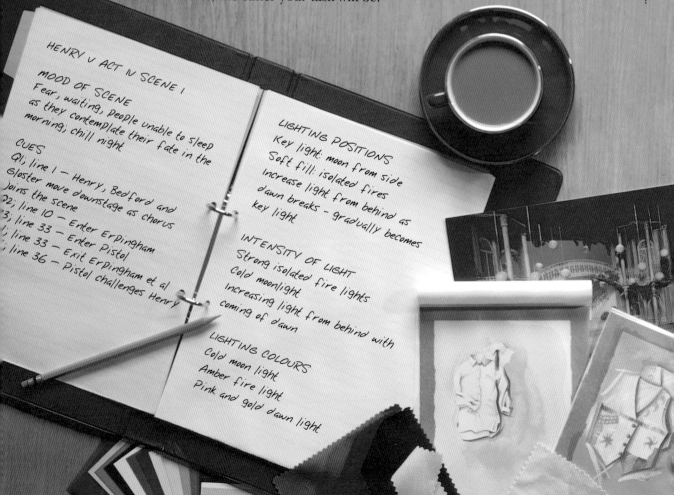

HENRY V ACT IV SCENE 1

MOOD OF SCENE
Fear, waiting, people unable to sleep as they contemplate their fate in the morning; chill night

CUES
Q1, line 1 — Henry, Bedford and Gloster move downstage as chorus joins the scene
Q2, line 10 — Enter Erpingham
Q3, line 33 — Enter Pistol
Q4, line 33 — Exit Erpingham et al
Q5, line 36 — Pistol challenges Henry

LIGHTING POSITIONS
Key light: moon from side
Soft fill: isolated fires
Increase light from behind as dawn breaks - gradually becomes key light

INTENSITY OF LIGHT
Strong isolated fire lights
Cold moonlight
Increasing light from behind with coming of dawn

LIGHTING COLOURS
Cold moon light
Amber fire light
Pink and gold dawn light

USING THE SCRIPT

If your production has any kind of script (remember there are many types of theatre which do not have a formal script as such), it will be the lighting designer's first point of reference. Interpretations of works may vary but the script is a constant point of reference for the whole production. So you must read it carefully! You should get a good idea of the plot, the characters and the general flow of the action; the key themes and the underlying emotions of each scene and character.

You may find it useful to draw up a synopsis of the play scene by scene, detailing everything that happens and noting any specific stage directions indicated by the author. Beckett, for example, was very specific in his stage directions. You should also note the time of day, location, and so on.

The next stage is to decide where you think the cues or lighting changes might come. To do this you need to recognize not only the beginnings and endings of scenes and the entrances and exits of the actors, but also the emotional changes in the action. Remember at the beginning of this book I said that the lighting designer has an important role as a story teller. You are helping the audience to perceive and be moved by the action on stage. It is up to you to look at the script and decide when and how you can best do this. You may find it helpful to use certain key descriptive words to describe passages, such as blissful, evil, deception, cruelty, defilement, jubilation and so on, to help pin down the mood of any moment in the play.

By summarizing the key moments in the script you can produce a kind of map of the journey the play takes. When reproduced as a chart using all the observations you have made, it will become the foundation on which to build your final lighting plan. Of course, your ideas must tally with those of the director and the other designers, but if they don't, the play map can serve as a useful basis to determine the areas of agreement and disagreement.

THE PRODUCTION MEETING

Right at the beginning of the whole process the creative team involved in the production should meet to discuss the basic ideas for the show. The meeting is generally led by the director, who will have suggestions, or even very definite ideas, about how the production should be staged. At this meeting your play map will come in very useful as a guide to how you see the lighting. The set designer may also provide a mock-up scale model made of card, which will be very useful in determining your lighting plan and pointing to any future problems. The idea of the production meeting is to reach a consensus on how to move forward and in what way.

Bringing along photographs and pictures to illustrate some of your ideas about how the production should look may help you to present your ideas to the director. These may in turn affect the ideas of the others involved. The best productions proceed through a continuous process of mutual respect and cross-fertilization of ideas.

The Set Model

After the production meeting and the initial discussions, most of the design problems should have been ironed out. The set designer will then go away and produce a scale model of the set which he or she hopes to produce. This will be a detailed model, unlike the first mock-up, and will be in colour, representing all the scene changes and large objects which will be present on the stage. This model is invaluable to the lighting designer as it enables him or her to see the shape of the production as well as the kind of problems it is likely to present, including the sorts of special lighting you might need – lighting through windows, for example.

Set models can vary from the very basic to rather elaborate constructions. It is essential that the lighting designer studies the set model carefully as it will have an enormous impact on his or her lighting design.

Rehearsals

At the production meeting you should decide how many rehearsals you might need to attend, though you can always come to more if necessary by arrangement with the director. It is important to attend the first rehearsal or read through, which gives some idea of the length of the play and where possible light changes might occur. You will also find it useful to hear the play read aloud. A good actor can make the text come alive in ways it is impossible to imagine by just reading it to yourself, and nuances of meaning may appear which had never suggested themselves before. This can be an inspiration, so make sure you go and listen!

Later rehearsals will involve the "blocking" of the actors' moves. This means their movements are noted by the stage management and so set for the production. It can be very useful to videotape these later rehearsals to use as points of reference later on. Theoretically, if you know the blocking, you should know where the actor will be on stage at any one time and so be able to light him or her. However, actors do sometimes have an unnerving ability to miss their lights and disappear into the darkness and oblivion. If they do, don't let it be your fault. At this stage the lighting designer can begin to assemble a list of cues.

The first read through of the script is an exciting time as you will begin to feel the production coming to life, taking its first faltering steps from the two-dimensional representation on the page to a three-dimensional production.

The Cue Synopsis

By now you will probably be imagining some of the lighting states you would like to see. You can use your play map to begin to produce a list of cues or a cue synopsis for the whole production. If you have been able to take videotapes of rehearsals, these will also help you to prepare the list of cues. Work out each scene on a floor plan with directional arrows indicating the paths taken by each of the actors. You can then begin to add in the suggested colour and light direction for each scene and each cue, using the text for reference. At this stage you don't need to note down any equipment as such, but it is a good time to start dealing with some of those problems which are just waiting to pounce on you. The work you do now will save you having to deal with them at the fit-up.

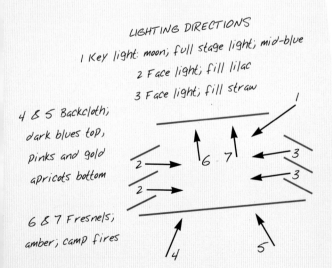

CUE SYNOPSIS
Q1. Henry, Bedford and
Gloster enter
Night sky background
Key light: moon light
Camp fires from
Pinspots: dim
Fade Pinspot on
chorus x 2 secs

LIGHTING DIRECTIONS
1 Key light: moon; full stage light; mid-blue
2 Face light; fill lilac
3 Face light; fill straw

4 & 5 Backcloth;
dark blues top,
pinks and gold
apricots bottom

6 & 7 Fresnels;
amber; camp fires

Once you have produced a list of cues, map out the directions from which you will light the scene. It is not necessary to show the kind of equipment that will be used at this stage.

HOW TO PROJECT LIGHT THROUGH A WINDOW IN A BOX SET

1. A box set representing a typical room will require diffuse light to be shone through a window.

UNSUITABLE POSITIONS

Because of the set or the shape of the theatre it may sometimes prove impossible to project light to the required area of the stage. You could solve this by taking a saw to the set when the designer is out of the room, or you could rig mirrors to reflect beams or projections, which is much less likely to get you into trouble.

SIDE LIGHTING

Some productions, particularly those involving dance, may require side lighting. This can involve anything from individual lanterns on tripods at the side of the stage to rows of lanterns on ladders or booms. Check that the side areas of the stage can accommodate all the lighting you wish to use, and make sure the booms and ladders are bolted securely at the side of the stage for safety reasons. You must also remember the performers, and provide enough room for them to enter and leave the stage without having to squeeze past hot lights. This is particularly important with dance. Dancers are frequently expected to leap off stage into the wings, and it would be most unfortunate if they were to leap straight into a lighting boom.

The booms can be masked behind flats or "legs" – cloths suspended vertically from the flies to mask the sides of the stage. If the legs or flats are angled slightly downstage, this will prevent light hitting the edge of the leg from the other side, so there will be no spill.

BOX SETS

A box set usually represents a room with three walls, the fourth being the invisible wall at the front of the stage. This means that all entrances must be through doorways, which restricts the amount of light you can project from the side, for example. You may also require specials to represent light through windows and so on. Sometimes, set designers want to add ceilings to the box set. Obviously, this restricts the lighting possibilities even further, so explain that it is better to suggest a ceiling, and ask for a lighting bar to be included somewhere in the design.

EXPOSED RIGS

In some theatres the lighting rig is not concealed behind a proscenium arch or masked in any way from the audience. If this is the case, the rig should be thought of as part of the overall look of the production, and is not necessarily a problem. Skilful focusing can avoid drawing attention to it. The model should provide you with a good idea of where and how the set or the shape of the venue might cause you problems, and it is best to approach these in the early stages and ask for concessions from the other members of the creative team if necessary.

2. To do this, position a reflective surface behind and above the window. You will need to experiment with the angle.

3. Bounce a beam of light onto the reflective surface so that it shines through the window and into the room.

Making a Lighting Plan

Most lighting designers leave this until about a week before the technical rehearsal, because the nearer you get to production week the more aspects of the production will be set. It also gives the set designer time to produce an accurate floor plan of the set. You must get hold of a copy of this as it will prove invaluable in deciding where you can put your lights. Most of the blocking for the actors will also have been done by this time so the shape of the production will, largely, have been decided.

By this time you should have a detailed cue synopsis and an accurate idea of the set and how the actors move across it. You will have noted the colours and effects you want for each cue, checked your lighting stock and become aware of the limitations of the venue and any obstructions on the set. Armed with this information, you can begin to draw up directional diagrams for the lights. Basically, this involves taking the ground plan and working out the approximate positions, directions and colours for lanterns to produce each of the states required in your cue synopsis. Look at the kind of effects you would like to produce from the cue synopsis, which you have been refining over the past few weeks, and try to express it in terms of lanterns and colours. You end up with a number of plans, each representing a lighting state in the play.

It is now time to produce the lighting plan. This is drawn on to a plan of the lighting grid using either a special scale stencil or the conventional symbols for each type of lantern. By doing this the lighting designer is fixing the design in a form which can be read and reproduced in the theatre. Each lantern should be numbered. This number refers to a master key – the lantern schedule – and describes the type of lantern it is, the colour it contains, the dimmer it is plugged into, what it does and where it should be focused. If your venue has a chief electrician, he or she should receive a copy of the layout plan and the lantern schedule at least a week before the opening.

The lantern schedule should contain an identification number, the type of lantern, the dimmer number, a colour code and focus information for each lantern in the design.

23	Parcan	19	181	SR blue back light
24	cyc batton	16	blue	back cloth
5	cyc batton	17	red	back cloth
	1lon	18	green	back cloth
		181	CS blue back light
			front CS red wash

Lantern number	Type	Dimmer	Colour	Focus
1	1 kw Profile	1	o/w (open white)	front SR wash
2	1 kw fresnel	4	117	front SR blue wash
3	1 kw Profile	1	o/w	front SR wash
				front CS red wash

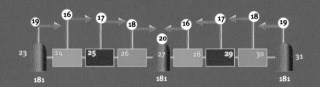

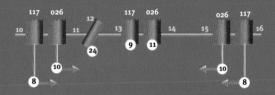

On this lighting plan, the bottom row of lanterns would be suspended in the front-of-house area. It holds spotlights to highlight the performers and fresnels to produce a wash of colour. The middle two bars would be above the stage itself and hold fresnels, again to give a wash of colour, and a special spotlight to focus on a particular element of the set. The top row holds parcans and floods to light the backcloth. The two sidebars represent vertical booms at the side of the stage with spotlights at head, middle and shin height.

Each lantern's identification number (as per the lantern schedule) is written at its base, its colour code at the front and the dimmer number in a circle. Dimmers control the power supply and there are rarely enough to use one per lantern, so the lights are often paired up to one dimmer, as indicated with lines and arrows. Here, those holding the same colour are paired as you are likely to fade these lanterns in or out at the same time. By pairing them, the person working at the control board will be able to fade them by manipulating one control only.

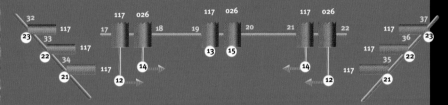

Manufacturer's supply stencils of symbols for their lanterns, which you use to draw your lighting plans.

KEY TO SYMBOLS

fresnel

parcan

spotlight, such as a profile or ellipsoid

flood

Stage Sections and Light

There are many different ways to light a stage, and different structures for lighting – back light, side light, front light, top light, and so on. All of these are at your disposal when you plan to light a production; there are no set rules for what works in any given situation. It is up to you to use your imagination and experience to choose the structure or combinations of structures which produce the most pleasing effect and satisfy the director. We have seen that lighting the acting area begins with the process of dividing it up into a grid pattern. Don't make the areas too small or you will end up using too many lanterns, and the rig will be a nightmare. Conversely, don't make them too large, otherwise you will not be able to light them sufficiently. As a rough guide divide the stage into areas 2.5 metres (8 feet) deep by 2.5 metres (8 feet) wide by 2 metres (6½ feet) high, and light each of these sections like a smaller version of the whole stage.

CONVENTIONAL LIGHTING DESIGNS

In conventional productions the actors are lit primarily from the front to ensure that they will be seen by the audience, from which direction the light will be coming. Each of the sections should be lit by two lanterns from the front, each at a 45-degree angle from the centre in both horizontal and vertical planes. You can further improve this set-up by pairing each of the lanterns and fitting two of them with cool tint gels and two with warm. Thus the "temperature" of each section of the stage can be controlled, and by using different combinations of these tints you can control the whole acting area. If your system is large enough, you can connect each lantern to a different circuit rather than pairing them, which means you can contrast each section of the stage to a greater degree, or use the lanterns in combination to provide an overall wash of colour. What type of lantern you use to provide this cover is up to you. As a rule, profiles are used to project light through a proscenium arch, but you must try out different techniques and see for yourself.

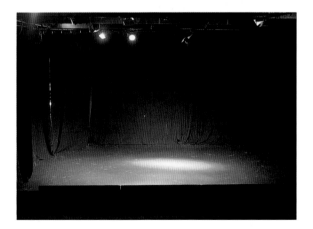

The stage is divided into a grid and ideally you should have enough lanterns to light each section as if it were a smaller version of the whole stage.

If a window is the primary source of light, place the key light here. Use a strong light source such as a parcan or profile.

The key light should appear to be reflected back from the surfaces in the room. Use a fresnel to produce this fill light.

LIGHTING THE ENVIRONMENT

In everyday life there is usually one predominant source of light which illuminates our environment, such as the sun, the moon, the light through a window, an electric light and so on. This should also be the case in creating effective stage lighting. You must decide where the major source of light is likely to be coming from. This main source of light is called the key light.

We also see light diffused around our environment by reflection and refraction from buildings, objects, clouds and so on, enabling us to see people or objects not directly illuminated by the key light. This form of illumination is called the fill light. On stage every light that is not the key light is a fill light.

Let's take an example. Imagine a room set with a large window at the back. If we take this as the primary source of light in the room, we will place the key light here, probably a strong, hard light source like a profile or a parcan. The key light here is a back light, and in real life would be reflected back and diffused by the walls, floor and ceiling of the room. So the fill light should be softer, and perhaps fresnels could be used from the side. Don't forget that the front light and any other incidental light also contributes to the fill. If the scene then changed to night and a lamp is switched on, this would then become the source of key light and the colour temperature of the fill light would have to change accordingly.

SPECIALS

A special is a lantern not included in the general rig which performs a specific function, providing a particular lighting effect, for example if an actor is to be illuminated by the light of a desk lamp, or if you wish to light an actor in a tight area and isolate him or her on stage.

LIGHTING THE SET

The final requirement is to light the scenery, backcloth or cyclorama. The set should be highlighted separately from the actors. You should be aware of the textures produced by different lighting angles and colours, and the lighting should enhance the colour and sculptural quality of the set and not contradict it.

Curtains look best lit from the side to emphasize the folds, but painted cloths are best lit straight on to show the painted image to best effect. Any seams or paint runs are then bleached out by the light and not emphasized. Gauzes lit from the front seem to be opaque, but they almost disappear when lit from behind.

COMBINING THE ELEMENTS

By deciding on the requirements for each of the sections above – the front light, the key light (side, back or top light), the fill light (side, back or top light), the specials, the set and finally any special effects – you can arrive at an overall plan for the lighting. Then you can decide on the colour for each lantern.

A standard lamp may become the key light in an evening scene. Such lights are known as specials or practicals.

An open door to a lighted room offstage can be an alternative source of key light, often producing a dramatic atmosphere.

THRUST AND IN-THE-ROUND STAGES

The techniques just described apply mainly to proscenium-arch or end-on stages. The thrust stage or theatre in the round presents a number of other difficulties. Most arise from the fact that the audience views the action from more than one side, and there is no or little use of a cyclorama or scenery. Great chunks of scenery on a stage for theatre in the round would obscure the view of the action for some parts of the audience. This means that the lighting designer has to lose some of the bolder strokes in the lighting design and go for more atmosphere and texture.

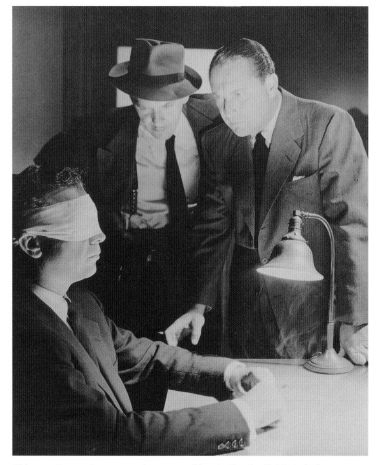

Old gangster movies are great sources of inspiration for lighting designers. In this 1944 version of *Farewell My Lovely*, Dick Powell as Philip Marlowe is isolated by a single light source as his interrogators peer menacingly at him from outside the sphere of light, giving them frightening shadows on their faces and distorting their expressions.

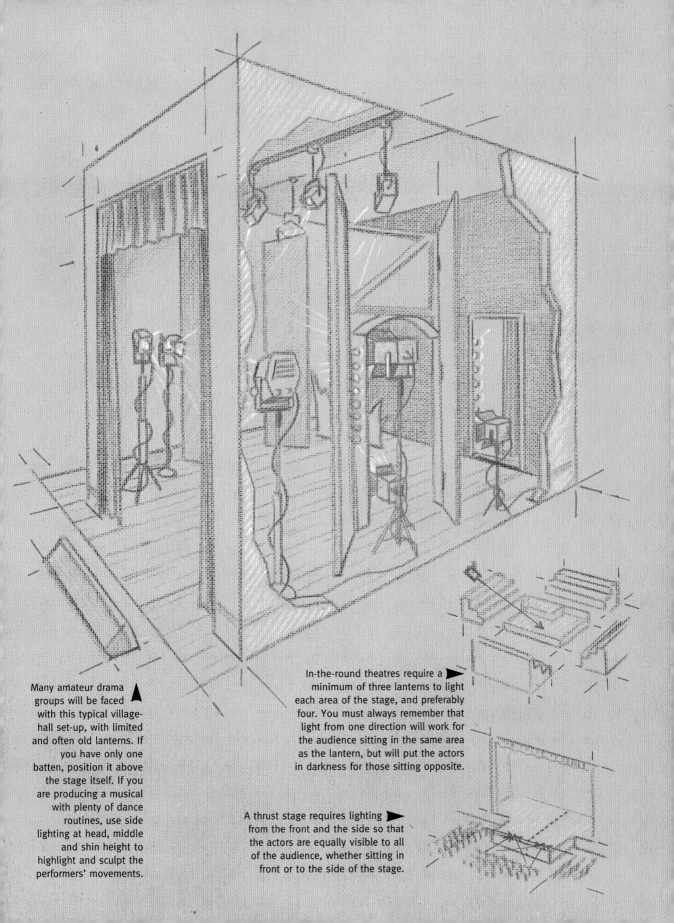

Many amateur drama groups will be faced with this typical village-hall set-up, with limited and often old lanterns. If you have only one batten, position it above the stage itself. If you are producing a musical with plenty of dance routines, use side lighting at head, middle and shin height to highlight and sculpt the performers' movements.

In-the-round theatres require a ▶ minimum of three lanterns to light each area of the stage, and preferably four. You must always remember that light from one direction will work for the audience sitting in the same area as the lantern, but will put the actors in darkness for those sitting opposite.

A thrust stage requires lighting ▶ from the front and the side so that the actors are equally visible to all of the audience, whether sitting in front or to the side of the stage.

Lighting Angles

Here we look at lighting the performer as well as at the options open to the lighting designer when positioning lanterns. This is worth trying out for yourself, just to see what effects you can get from positioning the lanterns at different angles and lighting from different directions. You can light anyone or anything from anywhere you like. The question is how does it look, and does it serve the production? Before you rush off to your nearest lighting rig and indulge in an orgy of avant-garde experimentation, let us look at the principles of lighting angles. It is again useful to divide the three-dimensional acting area into a number of directions in the horizontal and vertical planes.

The angle at which an actor is lit can dramatically alter how the audience perceives him.

THE TWELVE DIRECTIONS

This is just an expansion of up, down, back, front and so on. Let's start with the horizontal plane. If you imagine an actor or object which is to be lit on a stage, then you can divide the directions from which he, she or it can be lit broadly into eight directions. Although there are a multitude of angles between these eight, it is simpler to start by using these broad categories. In the vertical plane (that is, up and down) the lighting can come from four directions. Using these four divisions, we can describe all the possible ways to light the stage.

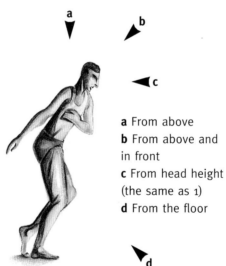

a From above
b From above and in front
c From head height (the same as 1)
d From the floor

DIRECTIONS AND COMBINATIONS

The way the light falls upon an actor or the stage can alter its structure profoundly, and the manner in which these lighting structures can alter the appearance of people or objects means that stage lighting can be considered a modelling or even a sculptural art.

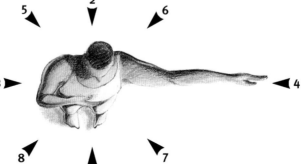

1 From the front
2 From the back
3 From the left
4 From the right
5, 6, 7, 8 From the four diagonals

LIGHTING FROM THE FRONT
A flat front light will shine directly into an actor's face and tend to flatten the features and look quite bland. It can be useful, though, as a filler light to eliminate deep shadows cast on the face by an intense light from a higher angle. All lighting produces shadows!

FROM THE SIDES
Side light helps to mould the actor's form and light him or her when he or she turns to face the wings. The effect of side light is to provide a dramatic modelling effect on the performer, which is particularly useful in dance. Beware of one performer casting a shadow across another though.

FROM THE TOP
Here the lantern is shone down directly on to the subject, creating a very dramatic effect, as the light strikes the most protuberant parts of the subject, leaving the others unlit. This can make an actor appear threatening and faceless or vulnerable and under scrutiny.

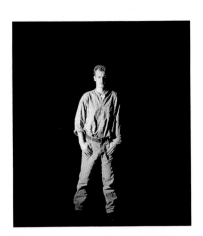

FROM THE FRONT AT 45 DEGREES
This creates some shadow and brings the actor's features or the contours of the object into sharper relief. If lit at 45 degrees to the side, this modelling effect is doubled and the subject becomes three-dimensional. By using both, all harsh shadows can be avoided.

FROM THE BACK
Shining a lantern from behind the actor and down on to his or her head and shoulders produces a kind of halo which helps to separate the actor from the background. It is a wonderful way to create atmosphere. Back lighting from the diagonal also produces interesting effects.

FROM THE GROUND
This is not considered to be a very natural form of lighting, but can be very useful and dramatic as it distorts the actor's features in a most interesting way. It is used quite commonly in horror movies. It is usually used to illuminate cycloramas and can create the illusion of a horizon.

Examples of Lighting Designs

Theatres and performing spaces come in all shapes and sizes, each with their own set of problems and delights. However, for the purposes of this book, it is possible to categorize stage and performing areas under three broad headings, as follows.

- End-on, proscenium-arch or box-set stages
- Thrust stages
- Theatre in the round

Sometimes the lighting designer will find that a theatre is a cross between any of these categories, or is a mutable space which can be converted to any of the above forms. In this section we look at each of the main types of stage area, and how to approach lighting it. Of course, each individual production will have its own separate requirements, but as you will see, each type of performing area has unique characteristics and problems. Remember, there are no hard-and-fast rules. You must experiment to see what works for you, and if you have limited equipment, don't be afraid to ignore all the "rules" and try something different.

Spotlights such as ellipsoids or profiles at shin, middle and head height provide strong side lighting to emphasize the shapes created by the dancers. This type of lighting design is used in conventional theatres where the audience views the stage from the front only and wings at the side of the stage mask the lanterns from view.

side lights   side lights

key light   back light   back light

side fill lighting

A strong key light from the left of the stage casts shadows and adds to the confusion of the crowd scene. With a thrust stage, the key light must be positioned at a steep angle to avoid lighting the audience sitting on the opposite side of the stage. The softer back and side lighting fill in the shadows to some extent so that all members of the audience can see the action clearly, regardless of where they are seated.

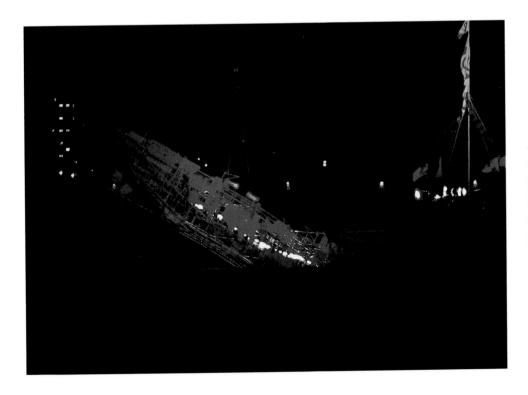

Theatre does not have to take place inside a building. In this open-air spectacle, the structure itself is the focus. Bright internal light sources silhouette its framework and the blue colour adds definition and a "from the depths of the ocean" feeling.

END-ON, PROSCENIUM-ARCH AND BOX-SET STAGES

This type of arrangement is probably the most familiar to people when they think of a theatre auditorium. The audience sits in front of the stage, which is usually raised above floor level. The stage is separated from the auditorium by an arch, called the proscenium arch, which contains the wings, backstage and onstage lighting. Some theatres have the same kind of arrangement without the arch to frame the performing area and are called end-on stages. They present similar problems to the proscenium-arch stage. The lighting for each type of stage with this arrangement depends on the set being used.

The lighting designer has the advantage of only having to light the stage for an audience which views the action from the front. Front-of-house lighting, side lighting and back lighting, can all be used to cover the area and light the actors. There are no problems until you add the set, which may obscure some of the angles you wish to light from. It becomes particularly difficult with the box set, which assumes that the action takes place inside a room, the fourth wall of which is where the audience looks in on the action. It generally uses naturalistic lighting, which on the face of it would seem to be trouble free. However, the flat surfaces of the set walls can present problems as the slightest mark on a wall shows up under the lights. You may also have to light through windows, and light scenery outside the windows, as well as providing a good cover for the actors. A box set may make side lighting difficult, so you must use steep side-lighting angles. A top light on such a set can be allowed a much greater angle and cover than the front-of-house lights, which light the actors' faces. Back light may be impossible due to the back wall of the set, in which case top light can be used as a compromise.

key light
through
windows

In this naturalistic scene, the light source would appear to be from the windows. The key lights would therefore be positioned here. However, with a box set, you may have to place the lights above the set and reflect their beams through the windows. Front fill lighting is also required to prevent the actors' faces remaining in shadow.

 front fill light   front fill light

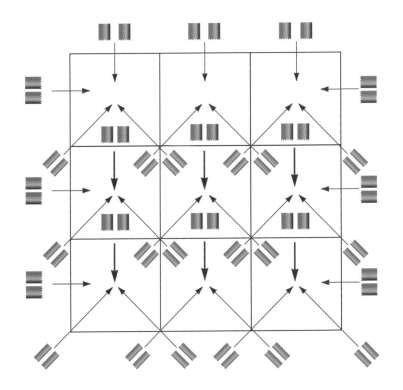

This lighting design for a conventional theatre (left) would provide perfect cover for all areas of the stage, with pairs of lanterns holding warm and cool colours. However, it would require a lot of lanterns. The design below would produce flatter lighting but uses far less lanterns. Putting stronger colours in the side lights would diminish this problem.

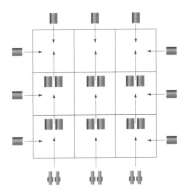

top light   top light

side light

side light

This scene is lit quite conventionally. The movements of the performers are accentuated by top and side lighting and the details filled in with light from the front-of-house area.

front light   front light

THRUST STAGES

The thrust stage has the audience on three sides. Often most of the audience is at the front, but this is not always the case. The general cover is split into areas, covering the acting space but often not the upstage area, which acts as a kind of backdrop to the action. Take care to isolate the acting area from the audience; as with theatre in the round, the lighting helps to focus on the area and make it distinct from the rest of the auditorium.

Each area is used for a different scene in the play, and they may not all be of the same size, although a strong central area, usually downstage centre, is isolated and highlighted. Various specials can be included for given scenes, using gobos or special colours and lanterns for soliloquies. Remember that there are fewer vertical surfaces to project on to with the thrust stage, and that badly focused lanterns may shine into the eyes of the audience. Because the audience is viewing the action from three sides, each special will require at least two lanterns to illuminate an actor properly.

The play of light down on to the stage is an important feature of this method of staging, so smoke can be used to great effect in making the beams of light stand out.

Essentially an end-on stage, this production's use of the central isle as a thrust brings the performance into the audience. Lighting the isle with profiles will create a controlled corridor of light for the performers.

A thrust stage can be lit in the same way as a conventional stage, but you must provide additional light from the sides and make sure that the lanterns are angled steeply so they do not shine into the eyes of those sitting opposite. On the illustration below, the method shown on the left is better but would use many more lanterns than the alternative on the right.

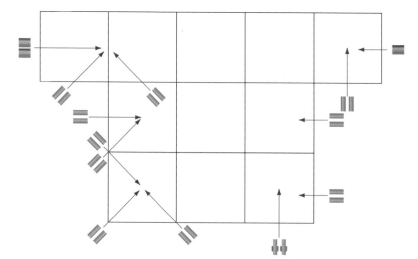

This scene is being performed in a theatre with mutable space, right in the midst of the audience. A general lighting stage is complemented with carried lanterns and follow spots to highlight the principle parts of the procession.

By using four pairs of lanterns for each area of the stage (below), you will be providing 45-degree lighting for all members of the audience, regardless of where they are seated. However, you can reduce this number to three pairs quite adequately (below right). Remember, steep angles will be necessary to avoid shining light into people's eyes.

THEATRE IN THE ROUND

Here the audience sits all around the acting area, and you must take even greater care to light the stage and not the audience. Because the action must be visible from all four sides, it is tempting to provide just two general covers using lanterns at 45 degrees. But this is expensive on lanterns, so three main light angles, each of 60 degrees, are used on each section of the stage.

With theatre in the round, and using three lighting angles, it is obvious that one actor's front light will be another's back light. This can make a considerable saving in the number of lanterns you have to rig. Check all the angles; you could save a lot of time and effort. Specials can be provided to highlight particular areas, but this time you may need three lanterns for each. The set must not obscure visibility from any angle, so vertical surfaces will be at a minimum.

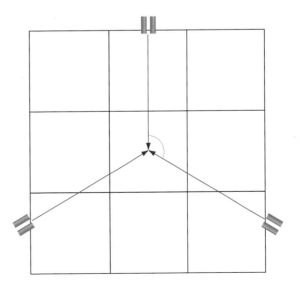

Achieving the Effects

Now that you have finished reading the previous section, you will have a good idea of a theatre's layout and of how and by whom productions are put together. You will be aware of the various stages a lighting designer goes through while developing his or her lighting design, from the initial read through of the piece to be performed to the drawing of the lighting plan itself, as well as some of the conventions for lighting the different types of performing space. By now you should also know the basics of electrical theory and safety. The next stage is dealing with the equipment which produces and controls the lighting of your production. This section looks at the types of equipment you may come across, how it works and what it can do for you. It also discusses the importance of colour and talks about how to create the right lighting atmosphere to complement your production, whatever the style of theatre.

The Luminaires

These are the names of the lanterns which produce the many forms of light. In spite of the vast array of lighting equipment available today for use in the theatre, the new lighting designer should not be daunted. It may seem a bewildering subject, and deeply esoteric, but don't panic! The basic design of every luminaire is the same: they all consist of a protective box containing a light source (called a lamp) behind which is a reflector which serves to strengthen the beam of light. At the other end of the box is a hole through which the light escapes. By placing a lens over the hole, the light can be altered, and by moving the light source in relation to the lens, the shape and intensity of the beam can be changed. The beam can then be shaped by irises, baffles or cut-outs, and can even be coloured – these adaptations to the basic box-with-a-light-in-it produce the different kinds of luminaire and their different functions. The main types used in the theatre are as follows.

- Ellipsoidal, profile and follow spots
- Fresnels and pebble-convex lanterns
- Floods and cyc floods
- Parcans and beam lights

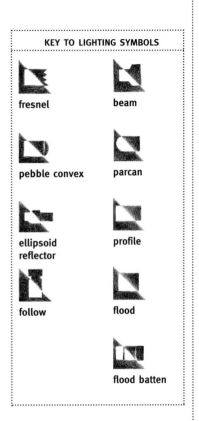

KEY TO LIGHTING SYMBOLS

fresnel	beam
pebble convex	parcan
ellipsoid reflector	profile
follow	flood
	flood batten

Glass lamp

Linear lamp

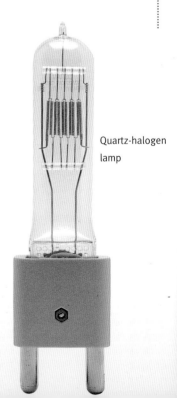

Quartz-halogen lamp

LAMPS

First, let's look at the most fundamental part of the lantern, the light source itself. As you would expect, the light is provided by an electric bulb, known as a lamp, and there are many different types. These lamps are made to take a particular amount of power, so a lantern designed to use a 1000-watt bulb will overheat if fitted with a 2000-watt bulb. On the other hand, if a smaller bulb of 500 watts were inserted in the same lantern, then the element of the bulb would not align properly with the reflector and lens system, and so it would fail to produce the correct beam. If in doubt consult the manufacturer's specifications.

Nowadays, the new lighting designer will most frequently encounter the quartz-halogen lamp, which gives a cleaner, whiter light than previous models. It is delicate, though, and even a trace of dirt or grease on the glass may shorten its life or even cause it to explode.

A lantern is a very simple piece of equipment. Light emitted from the bulb is reflected through the lens and onto the area to be lit.

These lamps must therefore be handled with clean gloves.

To avoid an electric shock, always unplug the lantern before attempting to change the bulb. When handling a blown bulb, take care, as the glass envelope may shatter. You should therefore use either a glove or cloth to remove the bulb.

The discharge lamp is becoming common in the theatre. Types include fluorescent lighting, metal halide, mercury, high- and low-pressure sodium and bulbs called HMI, CID and CSI. These produce a much whiter light than filament bulbs and are also more efficient, which can result in considerable savings. However, they cannot be dimmed directly by a conventional dimmer and require extra dimming gear. Because of this their use in the theatre is limited, though they are commonplace in television and film production.

Below are some examples of the lamps most commonly used in the theatre today.

Par lamp

Discharge lamp

Profile

Profile Spots and Ellipsoid Reflector Spots

These provide a hard-edged beam of light of a fixed size. The beam quality, that is, the hardness or softness of the edge of the beam or projected image, can be changed by adjusting the distance of the lens from the lamp and reflector. The plano-convex lens (flat on one side and convex on the other) is movable, either by adjusting a lens tube or in later models by using the adjusting knob at the front and base of the instrument. In later models there are often two lenses, which gives even greater flexibility when focusing. Light tends not to stray out of the edge of the beam because an aperture or gate is placed between the lamp and the lens. The gate also allows the insertion of gobos, which can be used to project an image in hard or soft focus. There are also four independent shutters built into the gate which enable the shape of the beam to be altered. Some models have another set of shutters placed away from the gate which allow the edges of a sharply focused beam to be softened.

This profile cross-section shows the position of the lamp, which differs to that of the ellipsoidal spot.

Lamp

Reflector

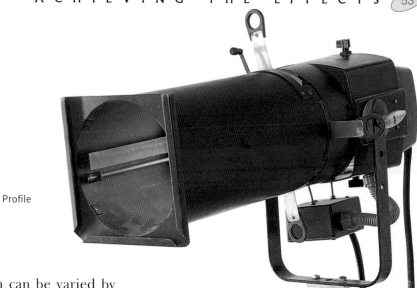

Profile

Lastly the size of the beam can be varied by inserting an iris into the gate. This works just like the iris in your own eye and on some models may be adjustable. The hard-edged beam forms a recognizable circle of light on a definite area, so whether used in conjunction with other lighting or on its own, it has a very strong effect, which may be used in many different ways; for example, to delineate an area of the stage sharply or pick out an actor in sharp contrast to his or her surroundings.

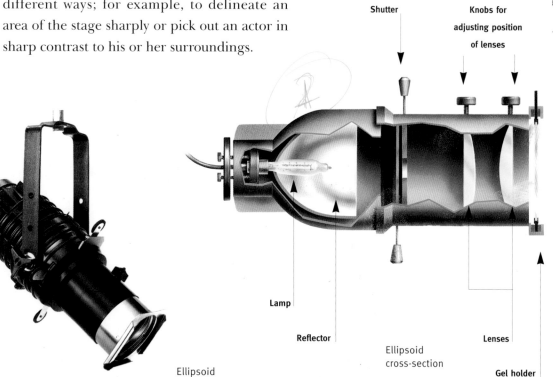

Shutter

Knobs for adjusting position of lenses

Lamp

Reflector

Lenses

Ellipsoid cross-section

Gel holder

Ellipsoid

LIGHTING FROM ABOVE

Mounted above an actor and shone directly downwards, the profile or ellipsoid spot can create a dramatic effect, placing him or her in a visible cone of light. When the brightness of the beam is lowered, the effect can be quite sinister.

HARD-EDGED BEAM

Profile and ellipsoid spots have lenses that can be moved close to or away from the lamp and reflector. When close, the spot will produce a hard-edged beam of light which will effectively isolate an area of the stage.

SOFTENING THE BEAM

By moving the lens away from the reflector, the edges of the beam will be softened to produce a circle of light with less defined boundaries. This will illuminate the scene much more subtly.

SHAPING THE BEAM

By using the shutters, the shape of the beam can be altered. It then becomes possible, for example, to create a hard-edged passage of light, or a square, triangular or trapezoidal shaped beam. Effects using the shutters can be projected from different areas of the stage – for example, from the side, above or in front – to enhance the drama of your lighting plan.

Follow spot

Follow Spots

A follow spot is usually a profile or ellipsoidal spot which can be operated manually to follow a performer on the stage. The lantern is mounted on a stand which allows it freedom of movement around the auditorium. An iris is usually inserted in the gate to allow the beam to be shaped and adjusted to the required size. Follow spots often have a flip-over colour changer or colour magazine to allow for quick colour changes. Specifically designed spotlights can be very expensive, so it is worth noting that any narrow-angle profile or ellipsoid can be substituted if an iris is inserted in the gate, but do remember that the casing of the lantern can get very hot. The spotlight may have its own built-in dimming system, but more often it will be connected to the control board.

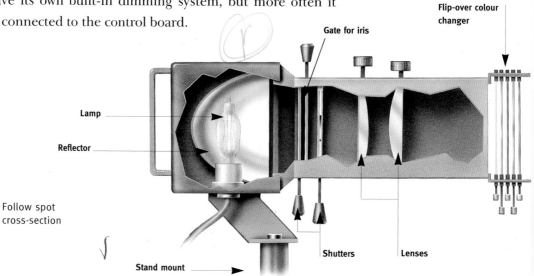

Gate for iris

Flip-over colour changer

Lamp

Reflector

Follow spot cross-section

Shutters

Lenses

Stand mount

The ability to isolate an
individual moving around
the stage is invaluable in
musicals, where the singer
often "acts out" the song.

Pebble-
convex

Fresnels and Pebble-convex Lanterns

The fresnel takes its name from its French inventor, who originally designed it for use in lighthouses. It provides a soft-edged, ill-defined beam which is varied in size by moving the lamp and reflector towards or away from the lens, which is plano-convex. The convex side of the lens, which faces away from the lamp, is stepped and serves to diffuse the light as it leaves the lantern. The fresnel is a fairly simple device which has no shutters or iris. However, because the beam is wider and more diffuse at the edges, it can be used to light adjacent areas of the stage as there will be no hard edges where the beams of two lights merge. The shape of the beam can be varied by using barn doors, which attach to the front of the lantern, in front of the lens and gel-holder, and act like crude shutters to block the light from each of four sides. Fresnels are usually available in 500-watt, 650-watt, 1000-watt and 2000-watt sizes. The pebble-convex lantern works on the same principle as the fresnel except that the convex side of the lens is stippled with small bumps. These diffuse the light to produce a semi-hard-edged beam which has no flare outside the beam and can be used as a substitute for a soft-edged profile spot.

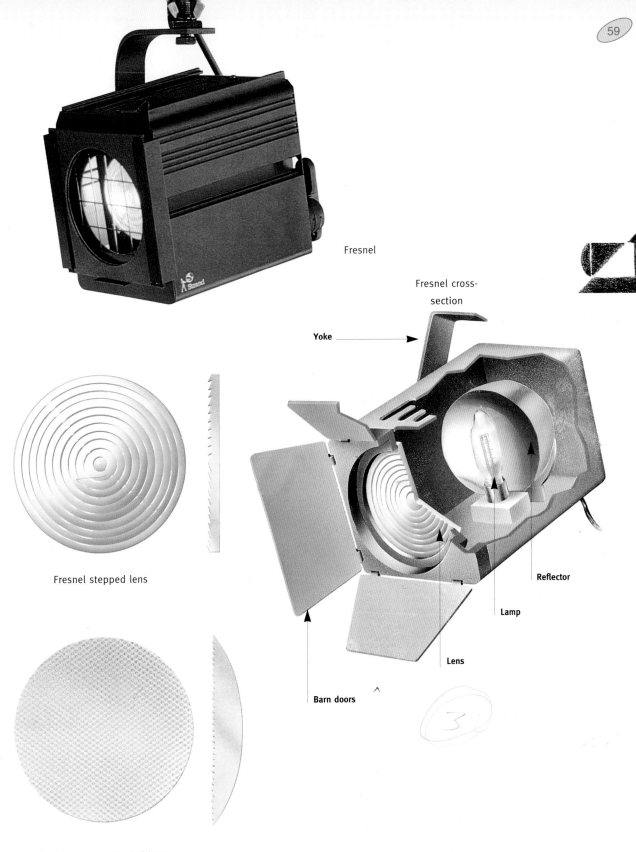

Fresnel

Fresnel cross-section

Yoke

Fresnel stepped lens

Reflector

Lamp

Lens

Barn doors

Pebble-convex stippled lens

LIGHTING FROM BEHIND

Lighting from behind with a fresnel or pebble-convex lantern can provide a very dramatic effect, but also some annoying shadows on both set and actor. Mounting lanterns behind the actor will place him or her in silhouette or provide a halo of light, which can be very dramatic. However, remember that if you wish to see the actor's face, you will need to provide fill-in light, probably from the front.

LIGHTING FROM THE FRONT

Lighting a scene from the front using plain white light produces an effective illumination, but is rather flat and uninteresting on its own. Combining front and side lighting will provide an overall cover which will light everything fairly evenly. Because the beam from this type of lantern is so soft-edged, the areas of light produced from individual instruments will blend into each other.

SHAPING THE BEAM

It is possible to shape the beam of a fresnel or pebble-convex lantern to some extent by the use of barn doors, which can be attached to the front of the lantern. However, these still will not produce a particularly hard edge.

SIMULATING DAYLIGHT

In real life, there may be many types of light entering a room, both diffuse and sharp. Fresnels and pebble-convex lanterns are ideal for producing a soft fill light to simulate morning sunlight coming through a window.

Horizontal batten of floods

Floods and Cyc Floods

As you might guess from the name, the flood is used to cover as large an area as possible with light, to "flood" the stage or light a backcloth or cyclorama evenly. Floods are very basic in structure, consisting of a lamp (usually a linear bulb, although older models may use a conventional filament bulb) and a reflector. Depending on the type of lighting effect you wish to produce, the reflector may be symmetrical or asymmetrical. The former produces an even distribution of light around the lantern and so can be used to flood a stage area; the latter is arranged to concentrate the light emitted at the bottom of the beam. This can be used to light a backcloth from above. Frequently floodlights using either form of reflector are fixed together on a batten to form a uniform strip of light which can be variously coloured. When such a batten is placed on the ground it is called a ground row and is generally used to light a backcloth from the floor. If it is moved to the front of the stage, it is called the footlights. These battens can be flown as well, and are then called magazine battens or border battens.

Vertical batten of floods

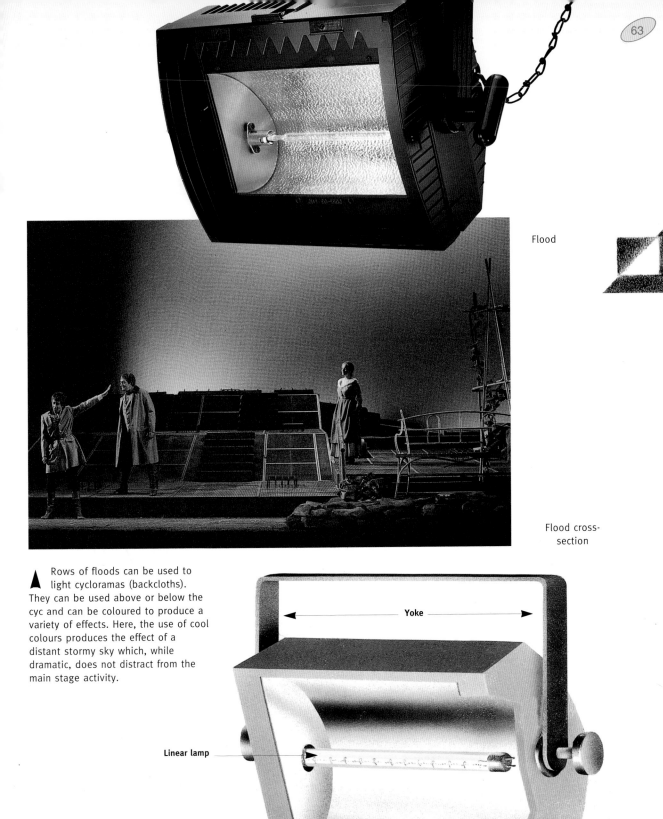

Flood

Flood cross-section

▲ Rows of floods can be used to light cycloramas (backcloths). They can be used above or below the cyc and can be coloured to produce a variety of effects. Here, the use of cool colours produces the effect of a distant stormy sky which, while dramatic, does not distract from the main stage activity.

Yoke

Linear lamp

Reflective casing

Beam

Parcans and Beam Lights

Parcans provide an intense, fixed, virtually parallel beam of light. Introduced in the 1970s, this type of lantern has grown in popularity and has revolutionized many areas of live performance. It is cheap, light to carry and quick to rig and focus. It is also particularly good for projecting deep colours. The lantern consists of a sealed lamp unit, rather like a car headlamp, which has a lens and a reflector built into it. They come in a variety of beam widths and intensities, each known by a different number, such as par 64, which refers to the diameter of the lens in eighths of an inch. The bulbs are usually either 1000 or 500 watts, and are housed in simple cases without lenses which keeps flare to a minimum. The parcan produces an oval-shaped beam which may be rotated or shaped with barn doors and coloured with gel.

Parcan cross-section

Yoke

Single unit lamp and reflector

Gel holder

Parcan

The intense, parallel beam of light produced by parcans has revolutionized many areas of lighting for performance. The ease of rigging and comparatively low cost has added to their appeal.

Parcans are perfect for strong lighting effects like sunlight, and have become the mainstay of lighting for rock concerts and dance. The extraordinary effects required by modern rock music are usually accomplished by using parcans. The beam light produces light of a similar quality to the parcan but uses a conventional lamp with a double reflector. Although largely superseded by the parcan, it has found much favour as a soft-edged follow spot, and, when fitted side by side with a number of identical lanterns on a batten, as a light curtain.

Controlling the Power Supply

If you plugged a lantern into an ordinary power socket it would work, but you would not be able to change the intensity of the light it emitted; it would simply be on or off. So theoretically you could run a lighting rig of sorts from an ordinary domestic supply in any building. However, most ordinary buildings do not have enough power to run the number of lanterns normally required for a theatrical performance, and there is the problem of controlling each of them and regulating the amount of light they give out. A theatre has a power supply sufficient to power a significant number of lanterns and the means by which they can be controlled in intensity, though the amount of power supplied will vary from place to place. As a lighting designer, you may have to light productions in far from ideal surroundings. Let us look at the question of power and control of your lighting design.

The mains power supply goes directly to the dimmer room, where it is distributed throughout the building. All lanterns are connected to a control board via a dimmer panel situated in the dimmer room. Information is fed into the control board, which sends it to the dimmers. The dimmers then adjust the power to the lanterns as instructed.

DIMMERS

Dimmers provide the means by which the lighting can be controlled. They are the nerve centre of the lighting system and connect the control board (of which more later) to the individual lanterns. Theatres have racks of dimmers located in a place that will provide enough ventilation to keep them cool and prevent the humming noise they give off from disturbing the auditorium. Each dimmer has a single or double plug to allow lanterns to be connected to it. This is in turn connected to a control switch on the board. The dimmer is where you will find the circuit breaker.

Older lighting systems use what is called an analogue control supply from the board to the dimmer. This means that each dimmer is connected to the board by a length of cable. This can prove very cumbersome and will limit the mobility of the control board. A digital system requires only one cable to carry the signals from the control board to the dimmer rack, and is therefore much more convenient. It also has the added attraction of being able to carry much more information, and can report back to the control desk on faults.

Most dimmers at present use analogue control. However, a control board which gives out a digital signal can be connected to them through a demultiplex unit (demux). Watch out for future developments; digital dimmers are being produced. The capacity of the dimmer should be printed on the case. Do not overload the system: a 2000-watt dimmer, that is, one that can cope with 2000 watts passing through it, will be able to power four 500-watt lanterns – no more!

There are numerous types of dimmer. The large one shown here is a permanent installation and would be hardwired into the building's power system. The smaller one is a portable dimmer rack, ideal for touring companies.

Controlling the Lights

The control board and the lighting technician are at the other end of the system from the lantern. The control board allows you to fade the lanterns connected to each individual dimmer up, down or out, so this is where the manipulation of the lighting design you have set up can take place. The control board can be manually or computer operated.

MANUAL CONTROL BOARD

The manual board provides a sliding knob or fader called the master or grand master, which controls the overall power level of the board. Then there is a fader provided for each dimmer and thus for the number of lanterns plugged into that dimmer. This means that each dimmer and its attached lanterns have their own individual control. The fader can be slid up or down to increase or decrease the power supply through the dimmer to the

This manual control board has two rows of presets, each with its own submaster. There is also a grand master which can override all the other controls.

Individual faders

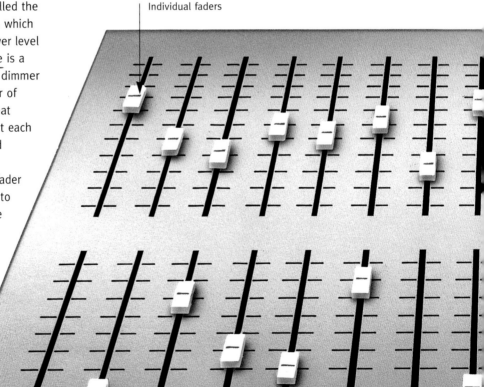

lantern and so fade it up or down. These controls are arranged in a row called a preset.

At the end of the row of faders is another sliding knob called the submaster. This can adjust the whole row up or down, so you can preset the faders for a particular lighting state and then gradually fade the whole state in using the submaster. This saves you the problem of trying to get all the lanterns for a particular lighting state at the right levels and on at the same time.

To facilitate this process further, there may be one or several additional presets, each with their own submaster. For example, if there are two presets with their own submasters, you can have one submaster faded up so that it is lighting the stage. Meanwhile, the second submaster can be faded down while you arrange the individual faders ready for the next lighting state, which can be faded in when required. Once the preset stage is operating, other lanterns can be added or taken out by using the individual faders on that preset, or indeed by combining two presets at the same time.

In the preparatory stages, the lighting designer will have decided on the levels for each of the lanterns for each stage of the production. To remember what is supposed to be happening and when, it is advisable to prepare a cue sheet, which will be referred to throughout the performance. While one lighting state is operating, the lighting technician will be studying the cue sheet and preparing the next preset, ready to fade it in and the other one out at the appropriate time. This is known as a crossfade. A manual board may also have switches for instant blackout or for timed fades and crossfades.

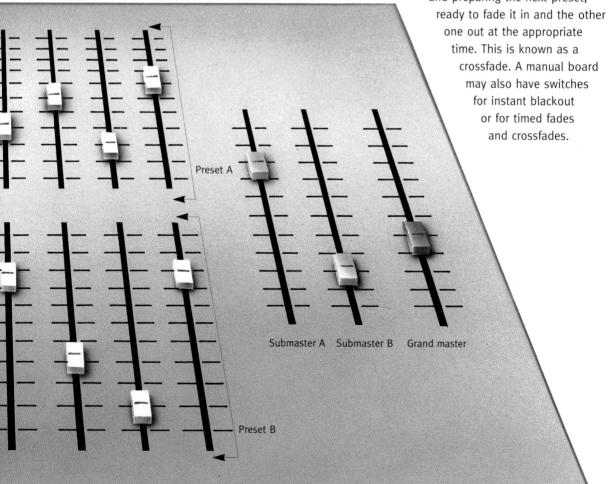

Preset A

Preset B

Submaster A   Submaster B   Grand master

COMPUTER MEMORY CONTROL BOARD
The introduction of computer technology to the lighting control board has caused a revolution in lighting design. It has rendered the cue sheet virtually redundant and made the job of the lighting technician significantly easier than in the past. The computerized control board can memorize a complete lighting state and play it back instantly. Each dimmer is assigned a number in the programme and its level is expressed as a percentage. Different channels are called up individually or in groups and their levels are set using the key pad or a master dimmer (generally a wheel). Once the level of each channel is set for a given lighting state, this state is allocated a number and recorded in the memory of the computer. Each state can be set to include details of the timing of fades, crossfades, the fading in and out of specials, and so on by using the timer function. This again is recorded and stored in the information for each lighting state.

The lighting designer continues this process until the whole of the design is finished. Then during the performance each of the states is played back by the press of a button. On more modern boards information on all of the lighting on stage is displayed on a VDU screen. Many boards incorporate a manual element as well for plotting. With this system the whole lighting plot for a show may be downloaded on to a floppy disk and stored to be used again in further productions of the piece.

Computer control boards have made the job of the lighting technician significantly easier but by no means redundant. A competent lighting operator will be able to take control should the action on stage go astray.

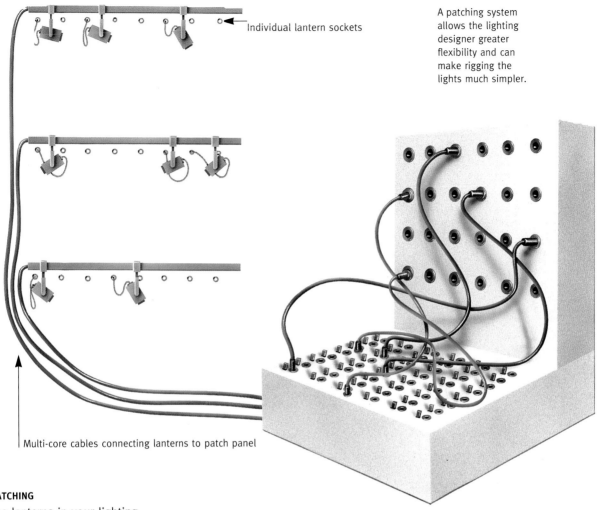

Individual lantern sockets

A patching system allows the lighting designer greater flexibility and can make rigging the lights much simpler.

Multi-core cables connecting lanterns to patch panel

PATCHING

The lanterns in your lighting design will be plugged into marked sockets by lengths of cable. These sockets in turn may run straight back to the dimmers or first run through a patching system. Each socket is connected back to the patching board and then to a plug. These plugs can be placed in sockets which are connected to the dimmers. Some patch panels have multi-socket arrangements so that a number of patch plugs, which are connected to the lanterns, may be plugged into one dimmer.

This means that two or more lanterns can be faded using one dimmer switch on the control board (remember to find out how many lanterns you can run from one dimmer using the watts = volts x amps formula).

Why bother? For a start, patching gives a system greater flexibility. You can have more sockets around the building to take your lanterns than could ever be supplied by your system. So if you have to concentrate your lanterns in one area, rather

than having to do long cable runs back to available sockets elsewhere in the theatre you can patch in the sockets in that area and run your normal complement of lanterns from there. Sometimes a complex production may require repatching during the performance. This can be included as part of the cueing and noted on the cue sheet.

Creating Atmosphere

Now you know about most of the technical stuff – how the lanterns work, how to control them, and how not to blow yourself up – you can progress to the creative bit. Lighting is as much a part of the theatrical production as the music or the script. Some people may think that stage lighting is just about making sure that the audience can see the actors and the actors can see each other and the edge of the stage so they don't fall off it. These things are all part of stage lighting, but they are by no means the greater part. As a lighting designer you should think yourself as much of an artist as anyone else involved in the production. The actors, director and writer are all concerned to tell the story on stage through the changes of emotion and shades of meaning which the human body, the spoken word and the art of acting can describe. The lighting designer tells the same story with the same emotional shades as the others, only she or he uses light to do so.

Light can suggest time of day, weather, mood, emotion, character, and even architecture and nature. The lighting state can be used to reinforce the action on stage as well as to set the time and place in which it occurs. It will serve to emphasize the style of the production and the story within it. If you want an example of this, look at the way light is used in film. How often do really scary things happen in half light or darkness? Or romantic scenes in soft light? Lighting can also suggest historical settings: think of the kind of shadows cast by candles in high-ceilinged rooms, or the colour of gas-light. Certain genres of theatre – opera, musicals, comedy, farce, and so on – tend to have their own lighting conventions, which have evolved over a period of time. These are useful to study because they often have a practical base to them. Although it can be as much fun to contravene these conventions as to keep to them, they act as an introduction to understanding how to light for the stage.

MORNING LIGHT
Sunlight filtering through a window can create a pleasant, optimistic atmosphere. Note the shadow of the window frame extending directly forward over the floor of the room.

EVENING LIGHT
Moonlight through the same window creates a very different ambience. Note that the window's shadow has moved across the floor to the left of the picture. This accentuates the movement of time.

COOL LIGHT
Lighting a room in a cold colour, such as blue, produces a cool, detached mood. A slow crossfade to this colour might serve to mirror and underscore a change in the mood of the performance.

SINISTER LIGHT
Lighting a set from below and in front creates shadows which can be quite sinister. This is very useful for illustrating certain types of characters, especially in melodrama.

DRAMA

This incorporates the whole field of theatre from tragedy to comedy, and from modern works through the classics to period pieces. There is no single established convention for any of these types of production, though brighter, lighter colours and less dramatic lighting angles tend to suit comedy and the opposites to suit tragedy. Light in drama is used to enhance the set, give depth and structure to the stage and to light the actor so that he or she may be seen. It is generally true to say that if an actor cannot be seen on stage then they cannot be heard. Lighting can also serve here, as in all other forms, to enhance the emotional content of the script as well as to provide clues to time and place. Works set in times before the invention of electric light may require special attention to colour, quality and direction of light, which can all serve to enhance the historical feel of the production.

▲ The cold light from the windows effectively contrasts the set and main body of actors with the richer, warmer colours of the main characters.

The strong, warm lighting ▶ coming from the right of the actor helps to accentuate the closeness, heat and tension of the scene.

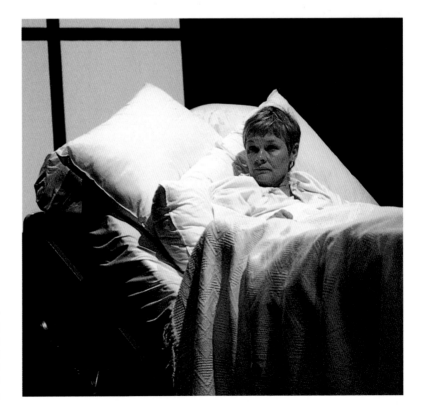

The harsh lighting is ▶ reflected by the white bed linen and nightdress, emphasizing the actor's smallness and isolation in the vast expanse of the sterile bed. Only her head and face provide a splash of colour.

DANCE AND MOVEMENT

In dance and some other forms of physical theatre it is not the face of the performer which is so important (although sometimes this may be the case) but the shape which the performer's body makes in relation to other performers and the stage area.

Lighting here must often render the performer's whole body visible. So side lighting is used in many productions, with lanterns arranged at foot, knee, waist and head height. Front lighting does not have to be so bright or specific as in drama, and back lighting can be very effective in picking out the figures of the dancers, as can the use of illuminated cycloramas and backcloths.

▲ The stage is swathed in a deep red light, which helps to accentuate the sense of danger as more characters emerge from the layers of thick smoke.

The mime artist's whole form is ▶ illuminated on an otherwise dark stage so that the audience's attention is focused solely on the physical actions and expressions of the performer.

▼ Side lighting is arranged in separate sections to allow the dancers to move in and out of focus, thus changing the composition of the picture on stage. Note the couple in the background; are they about to be the next focus?

OPERA

Conventions in staging opera
have changed dramatically in
recent years, with some of the
most revolutionary uses of stage
design and lighting in any area of
the performing arts. Traditionally,
the operatic stage would be lit in
parts, without a general cover.
Many opera stages are huge, and
so are the sets. But now there
are also many smaller opera
companies and operas which
require a different approach,
and a use of lighting more like
that for drama.

It was and sometimes still is
common practice to light the
chorus as part of the set. Opera
choruses are notorious for being
bad at acting (although this is
also changing) and a producer
will often want them to blend
into the background rather than
be allowed to ham it up in the
full glare of the public gaze.
Principal singers are generally lit
in a similar way to actors,
although arias are often delivered
downstage centre so that the
singer can see the conductor
clearly. Follow spots are used to
highlight the principals in the
larger, or more conventional,
opera productions.

▲ This grand operatic scene is very
easy to achieve: strong backlight
through the arch with a soft focus
follow spot to highlight the principal.

This group scene showing ▶
the male chorus surrounding the
principal couple uses the key
light from the windows to great
effect, but also requires a front
fill light to illuminate the scene
clearly for the audience.

Musicals can be amazingly glitzy affairs. Costumes, make-up, scenery and performances are usually strong and bold – so light the production boldly too.

MUSICALS

Spectacle is very important for musicals. It is often the glamour of the stage setting or technology which makes up for a lack of substance in the plot! Strong colours are generally used rather than the subtler shades which may be required in drama. The costumes may also be glamorous and should be lit appropriately to bring out the best in the colour and design. Follow spots may be needed for some numbers, as may specials. Dance can play an important part in this genre as well, and the dancers' faces may be as important as the shapes they make with their bodies. You may also have to provide special effects such as mirror balls or even helicopters.

Musicals are great theatre and audiences want to be "wowed" by the production. Swirling smoke, garish neons and strong top light produce a spectacular scene.

STYLES OF THEATRE

As well as the different genres, there are the different styles of theatre to consider. Dramatic styles such as realism, naturalism and expressionism set the atmosphere of the production and affect the way the actors perform, the costume design, the set and inevitably the lighting. As a lighting designer you should always look around for sources of inspiration. A great many ideas can come from looking at paintings, for example. A painter must decide on the direction, nature and effect of the light being represented as it is laid down on the canvas. The masters of figurative and landscape painting are the masters of light and colour. Paintings can also provide inspiration for historical settings, and show how light played on figures before the invention of electricity. If you have to set a production in the seventeenth century, for example, look at the paintings of Rembrandt or Vermeer.

In this ▶ painting by Vermeer, the woman is reading a letter by the light of an open window. On the stage, you would place your key light here. Additional fill lighting would have to be subtle to maintain the illusion of a pre-electricity era.

Photographs, films and TV are also useful sources of inspiration. As you watch a film or TV programme, try to see how it is lit, from what angle, and what are the predominant colours. Film genres are worth studying as well. Gangster movies, film noir, cinéma vérité, expressionism and all of the later genres are a rich source of ideas. Comic books and travel brochures can also be useful, as are the works of those other masters of light, the stills photographers. Last but not least is your own environment. Look at the changing light and the way it plays around you, and think how you might reproduce that on a stage. Be inspired!

▲ Genres such as realism may at first seem relatively simple, but it can be quite difficult to achieve the right colours and shadows.

▼ Film can be a good source of ideas. In this still from *Sunset Boulevard*, there is plenty of front fill lighting to highlight the woman's face starkly.

Colour Theory

We may think of light as being white, but white light is made up of all of the colours of the visible spectrum, that is, the colours we see in a rainbow. A rainbow is the visible effect of white light being split into its component colours by moisture in the air. Each colour of the spectrum has its own wavelength which stimulates the receptors in our eyes, and each is affected by mediums such as water, glass, air, reflective surfaces and so on, according to its wavelength. Objects absorb some colours and reflect others in differing amounts. So a blue vase absorbs all the other colours of the spectrum and reflects the blue wavelength of light, which our eyes receive, so we see the vase as being blue. The light we see is reflected and refracted from many different surfaces and through many different mediums, and so the colour balance of that light is affected. At sunset, light becomes redder; at noon it appears to contain more blue. A cave may seem to have a greenish atmosphere; moonlight is a pale, silvery blue. Colour also has emotional associations. Red is seen as hot, angry and dangerous; blue is cool or cold. The use of these colours can serve to underline the tensions which are being played out on the stage. Knowing how colour works can therefore be used to enhance your lighting design.

A cool blue tint from the left and warm yellow from the right help to create interesting highlights and shadows.

THE COLOUR SPECTRUM

If a beam of white light is passed through a glass prism, it will split into its component colours. Yet all colours visible to the human eye, including white, can be made from just three primary colours: red, green and blue.

The human eye has only red, green and blue colour receptors. To see the other colours, these receptors must be stimulated to produce different combinations of the primary colours. When all three primary colours are combined, white is produced.

Familiarity with this theory can aid the lighting designer immeasurably in deciding which colours to use on the stage. Certain colours will serve to enhance the appearance of dull objects, or enliven skin tones, but more of that later.

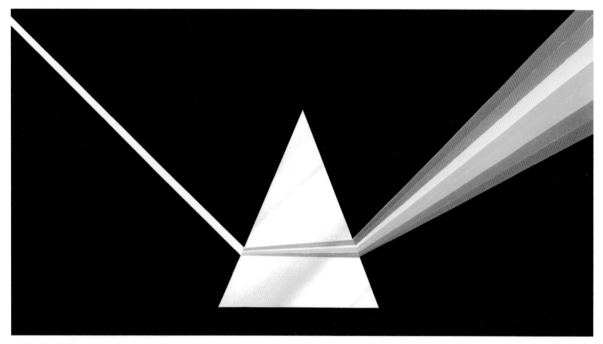

White light through a prism is refracted into its component rainbow colours.

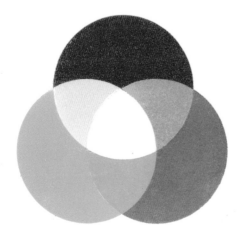

If two primary colours are mixed, they create a third colour. When all three primaries are mixed, they produce white light.

Under a blue light, this rose appears black; under a white light, it would appear red.

Colour Gels

First of all, how do we set about colouring the light from a lantern? If you look at the front of any lantern, you will see a narrow holder which allows a square frame to be slipped in front of the lens. The square frame is called a gel holder, and it is used to hold translucent, coloured plastic sheets known as gels. Gels are manufactured in rolls or sheets to standard specifications. Each manufacturer assigns a name and number to each individual shade they produce. These tend to differ from manufacturer to manufacturer, but they all supply books of gel samples, or swatch books, for easy reference. The gel is cut from the sheet (which should be marked with the colour and name using a wax pencil or adhesive label) to fit a gel frame, which holds it in position and will stop it curling with the heat of the light. It can then be placed in the gel-frame holder on the lantern. Gels work by allowing only some wavelengths of light from the source through. That part of the light not allowed through is converted to heat which affects the gel. Darker colours stop more light and therefore get hotter, which means they fade more quickly than lighter gels and must be replaced more often. Although gels are manufactured to be fireproof, the constant attack of heat from the light source reduces this quality with age.

Mixing Colours

We are probably all familiar with the idea of mixing together two colours of paint to produce a third, different colour. In the same way, any colour of light can be created using a combination of the three primary colours, red, blue and green (don't confuse lighting primaries with painting ones, which are red, blue and yellow). So theoretically it should be possible to fit three lanterns each with a gel of a different primary colour, focus all of them on the same spot and by varying the proportions of light produced from each, produce any colour in the visible spectrum. In practice, however, this is not possible for a number of reasons.

First, the gels that are produced are not true primary colours. The blue gel has to be darker than the other two to approach a true primary, and so allows through less light, which causes an imbalance. Then the light from the lantern is often not completely white and will tend to become yellower as the lantern is dimmed. This said, an acceptable white can be produced by this method, and if the shades of colour do not need to be too precise, then three-colour primary mixing does work to some extent. This method is most often used to light a cyclorama or white cloth as the colours can be changed so easily.

Don't forget that when projecting different colours on to a stage they will inevitably mix to produce something you might not expect. It is a good idea to experiment with different colour combinations to become familiar with the possibilities. You can also create other colours by combining more than one gel in a single lantern (useful if you don't have a full range of colour gels), but this will make the gel darker and so cut down the amount of light given out by the lantern.

SINGLE COLOUR LIGHT
Lighting with a single colour can produce interesting and unusual results. An overall wash of green light produces quite an eerie effect.

MIXING ANGLES AND COLOURS
A more naturalistic look is achieved by using two colours. Here, the stage is lit with green from above with a warm-tinted white from the front.

MIXING PRIMARIES: RED AND BLUE
Here, red and blue light are shone onto the actor. Note the range of subtle variations of pinks and purples that are produced.

MIXING PRIMARIES: RED AND GREEN
By changing the blue light to green, oranges are produced, creating fiery highlights on the actor's clothing and features.

Colour on the Stage

Now we have to think about how to use colour on the stage. We have discussed the use of lighting in different genres, the mixing of primary colours, the use of gels and correction gels. How do we apply this knowledge to the stage setting? First some basic principles: lighter tints are used to enhance skin tones and to lift the general stage picture. Remember, the lighting has to add to the costume and set design, not disguise it, so light and colour should be used to help sculpt the scene, by adding shadow and depth and livening up the colours. If you are providing a tint as a front light, for example, use a different shade on each side to mould the set and actors. If

Shades of blue and green colour and sculpt the muscle definition of the dancers while the central figure is highlighted with white light.

you only use one colour, you will tend to flatten the appearance of the stage. If the overall wash of the colour combines too closely with the set, it will appear "mushy" and bland. Remember your colour theory! Colours will combine on the stage to produce other colours. Some colours cancel each other out or leave a white light; others may change the colour of a costume or object completely.

CHOOSING COLOURS

You already know that if you mix the three primary colours together you will get white light. If you combine any two of the primary colours, you will get a secondary colour: red and green make yellow; blue and red make magenta; blue and green make turquoise or cyan. If you mix all these secondaries you will get white light. Mixing two complementary colours together will also produce white light. Complementary colours are a primary colour and the secondary colour produced by the other two primaries. So blue and yellow mixed give white light, and tints of these colours also produce the same effects. So by mixing a warm straw tint and a cool steel blue tint you will get white light. If you use this combination in lanterns on opposite sides of the stage you can provide the actor with a white light, one side of which is warm and the other side cool. This method of mixing colour using lanterns with gels is called additive colour mixing.

Mixing colours by combining gels in the gel frames is called subtractive colour mixing,

You can use bold and intense colours or subtle tints and hues. There are no rules so do not be afraid to experiment. However, always check colours side by side to make sure that the effect they have on each other when placed together matches your expectations.

because less light is allowed through the denser colour produced by combining two gels. When lighting an actor or object from two sides, use a different tint on each side to add to the sculptural quality. If you are doing the same thing with one colour, then use a different shade in each lantern. Generally it is safer to light with tints from the front. The heavier colours should be saved for back or side lighting. Sharp back lighting will help to separate the actors from the set and make them stand out.

Colour can have a dramatic impact, but the changes can be quite subtle. You can create the same dramatic effects with small changes in tone as well as big ones – it all depends on the style of the production and how it is directed. It is not really possible to give any firm advice on the choice of colour; it is a matter of personal taste and of the nature of the piece to be performed. When comparing colours, place them side by side so that you can see their effect on each other. Some colours appear to be warmer or cooler depending on which colour they are placed next to.

COLOUR CORRECTION

Although it may be possible to produce an acceptably white light when a lantern is at full power, as we have seen, when it is dimmed the light becomes more yellow. If the light from a tungsten-halogen lamp is compared with daylight, it will be seen as rather creamy in colour because of the temperature of the element in the lamp producing the light. It is impossible to reproduce the temperature of the sun in a bulb, so a lantern is not able to produce light with the same colour temperature as daylight. This can be problematic in film and photographic lighting where a good match with daylight colours, or the lower temperature colours of candlelight, for example, may be required.

Colour-correction gels help solve this problem. They can change the wavelength of light produced by a lantern and thus create an effect similar to sunlight or to low temperature lights. They do not change the actual temperature or amount of light, only its colour. The blue range of colour-correction gels increases the colour temperature of the light produced by a tungsten-halogen lamp and so gives an effect similar to daylight. The straw range of colour-correction gels reduces the colour temperature and gives a dimmer light, such as candlelight.

When lighting an actor or object from two sides, use a different tint on each to increase the sculptural effect. The colours you use depend on the skin tone you are aiming for, whether a natural tone or a deathly pallor.

EXPERIMENTS WITH COLOUR

● Try to experiment as much as possible to find what works for you. There is no substitute for experience.
● Try lighting an area in only cold or only warm colours, for example.
● Then rig a number of lighting states from hot to cold and see the effect.
● Then try combining them.

● Repeat the experiment with dense colours or tints.
● Try lighting a face from two sides using various colours and combinations: warm and cool, hot and cold, two different shades of warm, and so on.
● Try lighting a scene from one light source, such as a window.
● How does a single colour wash look on stage? How does adding other colours affect it?

● What is the effect of placing a lantern directly above the actor and shining it down?
● How does it look if you light the actor from behind?

The list of possible experiments is endless. But if you are fortunate enough to have a theatre you can play in, the experience you gain by doing this will be invaluable.

1. Cut out the required shapes from the gel. Lay them over the gel holder to check the sizes and shapes.

COMPOSITE COLOUR

This is created by cutting a number of pieces of gel to fit in one gel frame and taping them together. Usually, the cross-over of colours is in the centre of the frame as this is where the greatest concentration of light occurs. However, do not be afraid to experiment with other compositions.

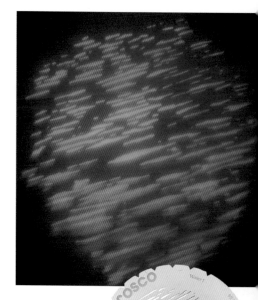

2. Carefully stick the pieces of gel together with tape.

3. Place the composite gel beneath the gel holder and trim to fit.

Composite colour gels are particularly effective when used with gobos.

Yellow light from the right evokes sunset, with long shadows. Blue light from the left lights the opposite corner of the room whilst maintaining the illusion that the sun cannot reach it.

Here, the blue light through the left-hand door remains, but a change from yellow to red creates a stark contrast, changing the scene from a natural one to something quite eerie.

Creating Special Effects

Amaze your friends and impress the audience with a fantastic range of effects, gadgets and ideas which can add an extra touch of excitement and professionalism to your production. A great number of devices available to the lighting designer can help to create the right kind of atmosphere. They can be expensive, although you can make some effects yourself. It is usually possible to hire effects machines from lighting-hire companies, and this is a good idea unless you intend to use the effect on a regular basis, or just like it too much to be without it. Whatever you spend or make, there is no substitute for sheer inventiveness. A special effect can be as simple as placing a light source in an unusual place. If a large box has to be opened, for example, placing a ground-mounted lantern with a coloured gel inside it, which can be faded up when the box is opened, is very effective. Add some smoke and it all becomes magic. Remember that special effects, like all forms of lighting, should serve the action of the piece, not dominate it. There is nothing sadder than a spectacular effect in a dull production ... unless it is a sad effect in a dull production.

Gobos

Stage lighting need not be just a matter of illuminating the actors and parts of the set. Light can be used as an effect in itself, or to create mood and atmosphere, and even become part of the texture of the set. The ability to colour and shape light which can be projected on to the set or stage can provide a useful tool in the overall design of a piece. One of the most versatile and interesting ways to do this is to use the gobo.

A gobo is a heat-resistant metal plate with a shape cut or etched out of it which is inserted into the gate of a spot light. The gate size of the lantern used obviously determines the size of the gobo. However, some lanterns are unsuitable for projecting a gobo as it must be placed between the light source and the lens. This has one drawback – the gobo gets very hot! Hence the necessity of making them from heat-resistant material. Lithoplate, a metal used by printers which can be cut with a sharp knife, is most commonly used to manufacture gobos.

The areas of broken light on the floor of the stage are achieved using gobos, creating the illusion that light is shining through the tree-shrouded windows.

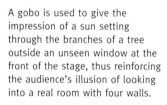
Venetian
blind gobo

A gobo is used to give the impression of a sun setting through the branches of a tree outside an unseen window at the front of the stage, thus reinforcing the audience's illusion of looking into a real room with four walls.

It is possible to make gobos yourself, although they can be purchased from catalogues or lighting specialists, who will have a wide range. Some specialists will even etch a design to order. It is worth mentioning that unlike most pieces of lighting equipment, gobos cannot usually be hired. The intense heat to which they are subjected means that they have a limited life. Do remember to check on the size and type of lantern you are intending to use before you buy one!

Gobos are not used solely for special effects; they are often an integral part of the whole lighting design. They can be used as an effect in themselves or to create textures, adding depth to a lighting state. Most commonly gobos are used to project images of windows, branches or leaves, for example, or patterns which break up the light on the stage.

BREAK-UP GOBOS

Break-up is a method of texturing light, which can be most useful in lighting a set or stage floor. Often washing a flat surface in plain light creates a rather dull effect. This can be greatly enhanced by using break-up gobos to light the surface, and soft focusing them so that the hard edges of the cut outs blur into a general texture. In combination with a composite colour gel this can be so effective that even the director may notice how clever you have been! A simple break-up gobo usually consists of a metal plate with a number of randomly spaced holes in it. A variation on this idea is the leaf design, which can be used to create woodland effects, or, if softly focused, can again act as a break-up pattern.

CITY LIGHTS AND SKYLINE GOBOS

As mentioned before, gobos can also be used to project images. Skylines of various cities are available, as well as city lights of many kinds. These can be used to suggest locations, for example when projected behind a window.

LEAF PATTERN AND TREE GOBOS

These can be used either to project an image on to a wall to suggest trees or leaves or projected over the whole stage to produce the effect of light filtered through a forest canopy. Used with soft focus, leaf gobos can also operate as break-up gobos.

BREAK-UP GOBOS

Break-up is a method of texturing light, which can be most useful in lighting a set or stage floor. Often washing a flat surface in plain light creates a rather dull effect. This can be greatly enhanced by using break-up gobos to light the surface, and soft focusing them so that the hard edges of the cut outs blur into a general texture. In combination with a composite colour gel this can be so effective that even the director may notice how clever you have been! A simple break-up gobo usually consists of a metal plate with a number of randomly spaced holes in it. A variation on this idea is the leaf design, which can be used to create woodland effects, or, if softly focused, can again act as a break-up pattern.

CITY LIGHTS AND SKYLINE GOBOS

As mentioned before, gobos can also be used to project images. Skylines of various cities are available, as well as city lights of many kinds. These can be used to suggest locations or projected behind a window.

LEAF PATTERN AND TREE GOBOS

These can be used either to project an image on to a wall to suggest trees or leaves or projected over the whole stage to produce the effect of light filtered through a forest canopy. Used with soft focus, leaf gobos can also operate as break-up gobos.

WINDOW GOBOS

These come in a great many varieties, and with the use of coloured gels can produce some spectacular effects. A composite gel used with a church window gobo, for example, can give the impression of a stained-glass window casting its colour shadow on a wall. Venetian blind gobos are also very effective, not only for suggesting, for example, a room in the tropics, but if placed in a spot light at the side of the stage and shone downwards along the wall, for creating the effect of shafts of light.

By combining a church window gobo and a blind gobo, it is possible to produce the effect of shafts of light beaming through a high window on to a wall of the set. This kind of combination can create startling and deeply evocative images which can be made to appear and fade in a way that static scenery cannot.

Some gobos can be used in combination to produce composite effects, though they must all be of the same size and projected from the same type of lantern. In constructing, for example, a stained-glass window, up to six separate gobos, each representing a different configuration of one of the colours in the window, can be projected from six lanterns on to the same area of the set and focused one on top of the other.

Break-up gobo

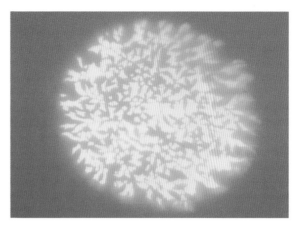

Foliage gobo

Tree gobo

Venetian blind gobo

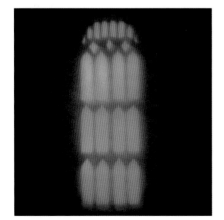

Church window gobo

Fire gobo

MAKING YOUR OWN GOBOS

If you decide to save money and make your own gobos, it can be accomplished fairly easily. All you need is some thin, aluminium-based metal, such as the lithoplate already mentioned, or, even cheaper, the base of a foil plate or tray, and a sharp knife such as a modelling knife or scalpel. First you must remember to cut the plate to the correct size so that it will fit into the gate of the lantern you propose to use. It is advisable to make the gobo slightly larger than the gate so that it can be moved and adjusted easily (but not too large to fit into the gate of course!). Once the plate is cut all you need to do is cut out the design you require. If you want a break-up gobo, then just drill or punch holes all over the plate. Other shapes should be cut out carefully using a sharp knife. Start from the centre of the design, and be careful not to go too near the edge or some of the design may be lost in focusing.

1. Flatten out the foil tray and use a roller to iron out as many of the wrinkles as possible.

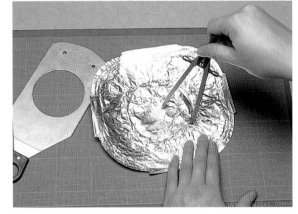

2. Measure the gate of the lantern you will be using, then draw the required shape on the foil using a compass.

3. Cut out the gobo with a pair of scissors. It is advisable to cut it a little larger to allow for mistakes.

4. Finally, use a sharp knife or scalpel to cut out the design you require. Do not go too near the edges of the gobo.

Colour Changers

It is possible to reduce the number of lanterns in a rig by fitting a lantern with a colour changer. The standard type is a motor-driven wheel containing five colours of your choice which is fitted to the front of the lantern. It rotates to change the colour of the gel in front of the lens. A faster and more sophisticated version takes the form of a magazine loaded with gels which can be dropped in front of the lens automatically. This is called a semaphore and can allow for subtractive colour mixing as well as individual colours and open white. Perhaps the most revolutionary device is the colour scroller. This is again motor driven, and it uses a continuous scroll of gel which contains up to 32 colours. It rolls the scroll in front of the lantern. Individual colours can be located in a split second by the technician at the control board, and the colour can be changed without dimming the lamp. It is a very popular innovation with rock concert technicians as it not only provides an interesting effect but also cuts down on the number of lanterns needed.

The standard type of colour changer is a colour wheel (top), which is essentially a motor that fits on to the front of the lantern and rotates a range of colour gels in front of the lens. An alternative is a colour box (above) where the different gels can be used individually or in combination, thus giving a greater range of available colours.

Chasers

Chaser units are found on many modern control boards and work by flashing individual or groups of lights on and off. They can be programmed to different rates of flashing, and have a number of uses. Overlapping flashing lights can give the illusion of movement.

Clouds

The most effective cloud simulations are those projected by a special lantern. These are expensive, but can be hired. The effect is produced by a motor-driven colour wheel fitted to the front of the lantern. This simulation works best if you use two projectors running simultaneously but at slightly different speeds. The clouds then appear to run across each other, and look more realistic. This effect can be projected anywhere you choose; experiment and see what looks good. You may be surprised to find an unusual way of using an effect which had not occurred to you before. If you are projecting the image on to a cyc or sky cloth, the effect is even further enhanced by hanging a transparent gauze or scrim in front of the cyc. The image will be picked up by the scrim which will also allow some of the light on to the cyc, thus producing a 3-D image. Static clouds can be created using meshed gobos projected in the normal way.

A moving effects projector will produce the most realistic clouds.

Moving effects projectors are expensive but can be hired.

Snow and Water

A moving, perforated wheel can be attached to the front of a lantern fitted with the appropriate gobo to simulate falling rain.

This gobo could be used to create the effect of either rain or fire.

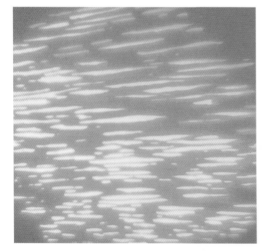

Perhaps the most realistic snow effect, and one of the cheapest, is to get hold of a large bag of small pieces of white paper, take it up into the flies and gradually drop it on to the stage. It will look great, but it will be very messy – the little bits of paper get everywhere. Then there is the problem of height. You need a tallish stage and flies to make the illusion work. If you have neither, it is still possible to produce an effective blizzard with a bag of paper bits and a wind machine in the wings. It is unpredictable but never fails to amuse the audience and the stage crew. Actors, on the other hand … The great Russian clown Polunin, in his piece *The Snow Show*, finishes the evening by setting off a huge wind machine at the back of the stage backed by powerful white light, and proceeds to blast the audience with a gale-force wind and bags of paper strips, against which the lone figure of the clown vainly battles. Fabulous! I have never seen an audience unimpressed by this, even though they may end up wind-blown and covered in paper.

Projected snow effects can be hired, although they tend to be rather repetitive. They work on the same principle as the cloud effects, using two projectors focused on the same area and run at different speeds in order to look reasonably realistic. Several water effects are also available. Running water and rain can be created using discs and projectors as for snow. Wave effects use pieces of fluted glass moving up and down in the effects unit. Ripples are created with a ripple machine, a rotating metal tube with a ripple pattern cut out of it, behind which a light source is placed, which shines out through the holes.

Strobes and Black Light

A stroboscopic light creates a rapid series of bright flashes, which can be effective in freezing movement or creating an effect like an old-fashioned cine film. It is also used to create momentary flashes of bright light, for lightning or explosions. Continuously flashing stroboscopic light can be dangerous, producing epileptic fits in some people, and there can be legal restrictions on its use. When using strobe lighting in a performance, warnings must be displayed prominently outside the performance space. Always take the utmost care if using it.

Black light is ultraviolet (UV) light, produced by an ultra-violet strip light. This, as you may have noticed to your embarrassment at a disco, only illuminates white or fluorescent colours. It can be used to great effect with puppetry or to create floating images, like white gloves. If an actor dresses all in black except for a pair of white or fluorescent gloves, only the gloves can be seen under UV light. Some companies have organized entire performances around the use of UV.

These actors have been painted with fluorescent and white paint, both of which glow under UV light.

WARNING

Strobes can cause epileptic fits

Always display warnings prominently

Find out what legal requirements apply

Light Curtains

Even if you do not have many parcans, you can use other lanterns to produce a similar effect. Here, a profile spot and a pair of fresnels fitted with barn doors create an effective curtain of light.

A row of parcans positioned directly next to each other, or a number of combined units using battens of parcans, produces a curtain of light. The beams should be as intense and near parallel as possible. The batten of parcans is then set at a steep angle towards the audience to produce a species of backlighting, but with the lanterns angled so steeply towards the stage, it is the beams of light which become visible. The light curtain picks up any dirt or dust in the atmosphere, further diffusing the light and helping the veiling effect. Adding smoke creates a very dense, moving curtain of light. Anything upstage of the light curtain is obscured, so it can be used to mask scene changes or provide a fantastic entrance for an actor who emerges through it on to the performing area. Adding more rows of different coloured lights in front or behind gives an even more stunning effect.

Moving curtains of coloured light produce one of the most dramatic lighting effects, which is why they are much used in the rock music industry.

Moon and Stars

A moon is generally created with an ellipsoidal or profile spot, using either a gobo or the iris of the spot closed to the correct size. This is then shone on to the backcloth or cyc. The lantern has to be at the right angle to the cloth to prevent distortion. You can add gobos to create the phases of the moon. This may be difficult to bring off in some theatre spaces where the lantern would either be too obvious, or would obscure the effect it was rigged to produce. It may be possible to hide the lantern behind a piece of the set, or to rig it behind the cloth and shine the beam through it.

A star cloth combined with deep blue light creates the illusion of immense space.

This moon has been created by placing the light source, either a profile or ellipsoidal spot, behind the backcloth.

MAKING YOUR OWN STAR CLOTH

Stars can be made in a number of different ways. You can project them with a star gobo in a profile or ellipsoidal spot, or use a star slide in a projector. Alternatively, you can make a star cloth by cutting small holes in a blue or black backcloth and inserting small bulbs, for example a string of Christmas tree lights, or the ends of fibre-optic cables. The latter are much the best solution and provide perfect pinpoints of light. They can be illuminated from a remote light source like a normal theatre lantern, and if used in combination with a chaser can even make the stars twinkle. A colour changer will produce an even more astounding set of effects. These days they are not expensive, but it can be rather fiddly work attaching them to a cloth.

A cheaper method of creating the night sky on your stage is to suspend lengths of black thread from a lighting bar and attach balls of screwed-up silver paper to them. You can make the stars twinkle by projecting side, up or down lighting on to them.

1. The easiest method is to use Christmas tree lights. Choose small ones and use predominantly white bulbs, although the occasional red or blue adds authenticity. Cut small holes in the cloth where you want each star to be.

2. Push each individual bulb through a separate hole in the cloth. Make sure that the bulb holder and the wiring remain at the back of the cloth and that only the bulb itself pokes through to the front.

3. Sew the bulb holders and lengths of wire securely to the back of the cloth. For a less permanent creation, you can simply tape them in place.

4. Hang the cloth and attach the lights to either a switch or the lighting control board. The latter is preferable so that they can be faded in and out.

Lamps, Candles and Fires

These are known as practicals and are stage features rather than normal theatrical equipment. Light boxes and stars are often included under this heading. Generally practicals are features which form a part of the set and must be seen on stage. Lamps which form part of a set can be conventional household lights wired into a dimmer and controlled by the lighting desk. If a lamp has to be carried, a battery can be used to power the bulb.

Flicker-effect bulbs can be purchased to simulate candlelight, as naked flames are dangerous and usually forbidden on a stage. You must take care to obscure the electric cabling and the general fake look of the device. You can make quite an effective candle using a length of white plastic tube with a flicker bulb mounted in the top and wired back to a power source, a battery if it is to be carried, or the mains. A wire is fed through a candelabra or candlestick and through the set, and when it is connected to the dimmer board the candle can be faded in or out with the general lighting. Dribbling white paint around the top of the tube creates the illusion of melted wax.

Coal or wood fires can be simulated by placing a light source in a stove or beneath a cover of prop coal or wood. It can be made to flicker either by using a slowly rotating wheel or by wiring a series of bulbs to the starters for fluorescent bulbs, which will flicker the bulbs at random. If your control board has a chaser, you can use this to flicker them.

This show is being performed in the round. The front rows of the audience hold battery-operated candles, which effectively brings them into the performance and at the same time isolates the actors.

Practicals are generally considered to be effects which are onstage and form part of the set, such as this standard lamp. An overhead lantern enhances the effect while maintaining the illusion that the light is coming from the lamp alone.

This candle is a made with a bulb wired to a battery in the stem of the candlestick. A candle light may need to be wired to the control board, for example if the candle is to appear to blow out in a gust of wind, but usually a switch will do.

MAKING YOUR OWN CANDLE LIGHTS

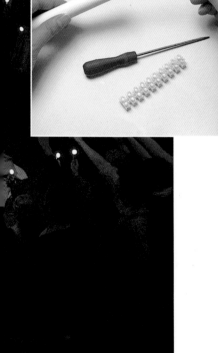

1. Insert a store-bought bulb fitting into the end of a plain tube so that the wiring extends from the opposite end. The wires can be connected to a battery as required.

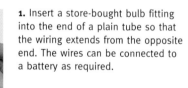

2. Make the tube look more realistic by dripping melted wax on to it. Take care when doing this, both to avoid burns and to avoid getting any wax on the bulb fitting.

3. Once the wax has dried, insert a flicker bulb into the bulb fitting.

Projections

Many of the effects already discussed are created by projecting images on to the set or backcloth. But projecting images can be a problem. Anything or anybody who gets in the way will also be projected on to, so unless you banish actors from your set completely (which some lighting designers would be only too happy to do), you must position the projectors very carefully. You can, of course, project slides on to an actor to create a special effect. One I particularly liked was projecting a loop of scratched colour film on to the face of an actor as he spoke. Remember, however, that projecting scenery is a particular style of design and should be treated as such, and not as a way of solving problems of scene-changing.

Unless the projector is placed at right angles to the surface it is projecting on to, the image will be distorted. You may need counter-distorted artwork to combat this. Ideally, proper projection screen material should be used because it will produce the brightest image, but any opaque surface can be used, including smoke, the set, an actor and so on. Back projection, that is placing the projector behind the screen, can solve some of the problems of avoiding the actors on stage, but finding the necessary space to allow the correct size of image to be projected can be a problem. You should use special back-projection screen material. A word of warning: do tell the backstage crew not to walk through the beam!

The swirling image and hand shadows are projected on to the backcloth from behind. You would need quite a lot of space behind the stage area to project an image of this size.

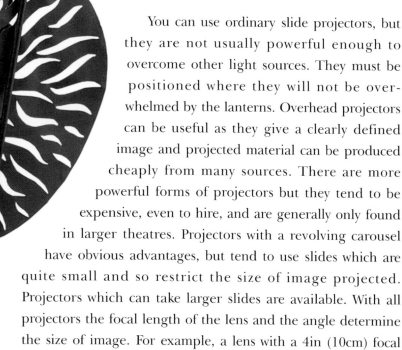

An effects disc fitted to the front of a lantern containing a composite colour gel ...

... projects a wonderful fire effect on to the set.

You can use ordinary slide projectors, but they are not usually powerful enough to overcome other light sources. They must be positioned where they will not be over-whelmed by the lanterns. Overhead projectors can be useful as they give a clearly defined image and projected material can be produced cheaply from many sources. There are more powerful forms of projectors but they tend to be expensive, even to hire, and are generally only found in larger theatres. Projectors with a revolving carousel have obvious advantages, but tend to use slides which are quite small and so restrict the size of image projected. Projectors which can take larger slides are available. With all projectors the focal length of the lens and the angle determine the size of image. For example, a lens with a 4in (10cm) focal length will be capable of projecting a 10ft sq ($0.95m^2$) image at 12ft (3.65m). Wider angle lenses will produce a wider image but may cause distortion at the sides. The subject of projection can be discussed endlessly and is fraught with difficulties, but its use can be very effective.

A projector is essentially a motor which fits on to the front of a lantern. Different types of disc can be inserted which the motor rotates in front of the light source.

Scrims

Scrims are gauze-like curtains which, if used creatively, can almost magically transform scenes. When lit from the front, scrims appear opaque and anything upstage of them will be invisible to the audience, but when there is lighting behind but not on them, they become transparent. You can make a scene appear by lowering the lights on the scrim and raising them on the scene behind it. Moreover, they can be painted. A room set used for a recent production had one wall made of gauze and painted to match the rest of the walls. Under normal lighting the set appeared to be quite solid, but with a change of lighting the events in the next room could be witnessed by the audience as the characters continued their dialogue unaware. Scrims can also be made translucent so that the audience can see the scrim as well as what is happening behind it. This is achieved by using some illumination on the scrim together with some lighting behind it, in the proper proportions.

A scrim is a gauze screen which can be painted to look like a solid piece of scenery. When lit from the front, as illustrated here, it will appear opaque to the audience and can therefore represent a brick wall, for example.

If a separate scene is placed behind the scrim, it will remain unseen whilst the front of the scrim is lit. As soon as the lights are brought up on the scene behind the scrim, however, it will become visible through the seemingly solid wall.

Smoke

Much beloved by rock stars and horror movie directors, smoke can give texture to the stage set and create atmosphere, as well as represent obvious effects such as fire or fog. Subtle use of smoke can reveal beams of light, create coloured mists or soften atmospheres. It is often used in film to give a soft, diffused feel to daylight in a room. The smoke is produced by vaporizing a glycol fluid in a heater. The chemicals are harmless and the smoke produced is non-irritant, but you can bet if any leaks from the stage into the audience a few hypochondriacs will cough! Many places have restrictions on the amount of smoke which can be let into the auditorium, though a mist of smoke in the auditorium, aided by subtle lighting, can create a wonderful atmosphere for an audience to enter. Smoke by nature rises and disperses, and the dispersal is greatly increased by an air-conditioning system. If you want smoke that flows across the floor, then dry ice is the stuff to use. Dry ice is solid carbon dioxide and is cold enough to give severe burns, so handle with care. When it is placed in water, it boils and produces a thick vapour, which is what you see swirling round tombstones in vampire films, or bubbling out of glass flasks in the laboratories of mad scientists. It is safe and non-irritant, although in excess it can cause suffocation. It can also – and this may be worse than suffocation to an actor – completely obscure anyone on stage if used in too large a quantity.

Smoke can help to accentuate lighting effects dramatically. Here, the shaft of light projected through the window from behind and above the stage appears almost concrete.

Smoke machines such as this one can be hired. Unless you intend to use one a great deal, hiring is probably the best option.

Light Boxes

These are simply sources of light contained in boxes. Any shape which is required can be cut out of the front of the box and then covered inside with a gel or a diffusing material to create the desired colours. Light boxes can be used to make a moon, sun or neon lights, for example. The type of lamp used is determined by the depth of the box and the brightness desired. For a shallow box, neon strip light is best. Deeper boxes can use normal domestic light bulbs, although these will tend to form hot spots on the surface of the box. Silver-topped bulbs help to prevent this to some extent. The light may be diffused by fixing a length of calico or translucent perspex over the surface of the box. A cut-out of wood or cardboard is then placed over the top of this.

For a moon effect, cut out a circle or crescent shape and place it on the front of the box and position this behind the cyclorama or backcloth, right up against the cloth to create a sharp image. A sun effect can be created in the same way using different colour tints. You can also suspend the box from a wire so that it can be lowered across the back of the cyclorama, giving the effect of a setting sun or moon. For a neon sign, cut the front of the box to represent the desired sign, then fix gel to the back to give colour to the sign. Different coloured bulbs can also be used; if wired to different circuits, they can be made to flash in order.

1 To make a neon sign simply fix a light source, such as rows of bulbs or a neon strip, inside a box. Place a piece of perspex over the top of the box to diffuse the light. Add a sheet of gel if a colored light is required.

2 Make a stencil from a piece of opaque paper by cutting out the required letters or design. Place this on top of the perspex. The light source inside the box will shine through the cut-out letters to create the effect of a neon sign.

Unusual Lighting Positions

You can create startling and beautiful effects by placing lights in unusual places. These can take the form of onstage practicals, like placing a light and a battery in a hollow in a book. If, for example, this were a book of fairy tales, to be opened by a child in bed late at night, the magic fairy tale book will seem to give off a strange light which illuminates the child's face. Lights which use smaller mercury batteries can even be used inside an actor's mouth. They must be well protected, as the contents of the battery are poisonous and the glass of the bulb could be dangerous. The same lights can be used in glasses or cups to provide strange sources of lighting for the actors. Lighting through less obvious parts of the set can cast unusual shadows. I have seen a single, naked light bulb on the end of a long cable swung backwards and forwards across a stage to great effect. Try lighting from directly above or below a subject. Have fun and explore your own inventiveness. Many productions have used TV and pre-recorded video tapes as well as live video cameras. Remember not to overburden yourself or your venue with technology, though, which might get in the way of the production. When it works, however, it is truly impressive.

▲ Lights shone through a coloured, transparent cone of material from its base up towards the performer give the fabric a substance it would otherwise lack and provide spectacular colour contrasts both with the performer and the rest of the stage.

The vibrant blues and deep ▶ shadows of this lighting design create a truly stunning visual impact.

Pyrotechnics

These devices deal with potentially dangerous things like controlled explosions, so they must be treated with respect. Any authorities which have control over your theatre will have strict rules on the use of pyrotechnics, often including a requirement to view the firing of the device prior to granting a licence for its use in a public entertainment building.

A word here about safety regulations and the bodies that enforce them. It may be irksome on occasions to have an official tell you that you cannot use a particular effect, or that you must fireproof your entire set, or any number of other things which may seem petty. But these rules are made, often in the light of bitter experience, to safeguard not only your life, but those of your actors and fellow theatre workers as well as the public. A theatre is a potentially dangerous place; adherence to safety regulations at all levels makes it a good deal safer.

Here are some safety rules about pyrotechnics:
• Do not keep large stocks of explosives anywhere in the theatre building. Any explosives stored should be kept in a locked metal cabinet away from possible sources of fire or sparks.
• Explosives should be moved in a portable, lockable, metal box.
• Never smoke while handling pyrotechnics.
• Load pyrotechnics at the last possible moment, but always with great care.
• A firing box must have a lockable switch as well as the regular one. Only the pyro-technician should have the key, and he or she should check that the switches are turned and locked off before loading the device.

A bomb tank is required for safety reasons but also provides that special echoey sound for realistic explosions.

A confetti canon will spray confetti all over the set – remember the clean up!

• The person detonating the device should be the one closest to it, with the clearest view of it.

• Remember during rehearsals to warn the cast and crew of the impending conflagration *before you set it off*.

MAROONS

These are basically firecrackers which create the sound of an explosion, by exploding! They come in various sizes and with various noises, and should be detonated in a regulation bomb tank – a one-piece, cast-metal tank, open at the top. Some bomb tanks have compartments to take more than one maroon, and keep them isolated so they do not set each other off. The top of the tank should be covered with mesh to prevent any pieces of maroon from escaping during the explosion, but do NOT cover the tank completely as you will make it into a bomb! The maroon is detonated by a special detonator which can be run from a six-volt battery.

FLASHES

These used to be produced using flash powder, which was a laborious and precarious undertaking. Now you can buy pre-made cartridge systems and pyro-fuses. The cartridge is placed in a pyro-box which is connected to a firing box and so to the power supply. Flashes come in a wide variety of effects and can be great fun.

STREAMERS

These are available in cartridge form and are detonated using the same system as that used for flashes. They include glitter and confetti cannons.

Five flame projectors are set off at once here. You must take great care if using an effect such as this.

Maroons come in various sizes and must be exploded in a bomb tank.

Flash and flame projectors are most commonly used at rock concerts.

Glitter cartridges are wonderfully effective at children's shows.

Production

You have now learned all about the pre-planning stage involved in lighting a theatrical production, and you should also be aware of the various items of equipment at your disposal and what you can do with them. You will have spent some time experimenting with the various effects you want to produce, and you will have decided on any special effects required and arranged to hire or buy the necessary equipment. Now comes the production week, when you actually take your °ideas into the theatre. You will have produced your lighting plan and some of it may have already been set up by the electrical staff at the venue. During the production week the whole piece will be assembled. The week culminates in the opening night of the show. Your work does not end there, however, as you must make sure that everything continues to run smoothly and as planned. If the production is touring, you must also be prepared to make changes to the design if required as you go from venue to venue.

Planning

The production week is a time of hectic activity and careful planning is essential. It is during this period that the lighting designer refines his or her design and draws together the necessary equipment and information, including how long is available to "fit up" or "rig", and how long might actually be needed.

You must distribute copies of the lighting plan to all who need to see it, including the electric's team and any other relevant part of the production team. Make sure you order the colour gels for the production well in advance as you may have difficulty in obtaining all the required colours. Order more than you think you need if you can afford it, to ensure you are covered if you run out or need more of a colour than you thought, or if somebody walks off with some of your stock. Each colour should be cut to size for the required lantern, placed in an individual envelope, and numbered and labelled according to its location in the rig. This preparation will save a lot of time when fitting-up.

Check your stock of equipment and materials well in advance, and always make sure that they are functioning as required.

Study your lighting plan and work out how many adapters you will need for paired lanterns and that the cable you are going to use is the correct size. Check the hire equipment to see that it is what you ordered and that it is working. If any piece of equipment requires special cabling, check that this has been included, and that any spare bulbs are sound. Make sure you have a supply of spare fuses. Last, but by no means least, lay in a good stock of gaffer tape, which is possibly the single most useful invention in theatrical history.

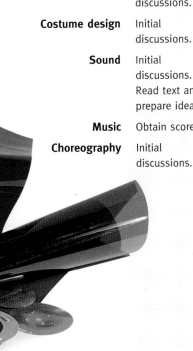

PRODUCTION SCHEDULE

PREPARATION: WEEK 12

Lighting	Script preparation.
Director	Pre-production discussions. Auditions. Prepare audition schedules.
Administration	Prepare budget. Check performance and copyright issues and royalty payments. Find venue and performance window. Initial discussions.
Production manager	Discuss budget with admin. Hire stage management and technical staff.
Set design	Initial discussions.
Costume design	Initial discussions.
Sound	Initial discussions. Read text and prepare ideas.
Music	Obtain scores.
Choreography	Initial discussions.

PREPARATION: WEEK 11

Lighting	Script preparation.
Director	As above.
Administration	Ideas for publicity. Call auditions.
Production manager	As above.
Sound	Provisional recording.
Music	Auditions.
Choreography	Auditions.

PREPARATION: WEEK 10

Lighting	Research. Meet director, set and costume designers.
Director	Auditions.
Administration	Plan publicity.
Production manager	Design meeting.
Stage management	Design meeting. Run auditions. Research with designer.
Set design	Design meeting.
Costume design	Design meeting.
Sound	Preparation of provisional tapes and discussion with director.

The length of production schedules can vary a great deal from company to company. The example shown in this section assumes a production period of twelve weeks. Bear in mind that this could be considerably shorter and there may be far less people involved, depending on your budget.

THE TEAM

It would be very hard work, and probably dangerous, to set up a lighting rig on your own. So you need to work with a group of people to help you realize the design. These will sometimes be part of the electrical staff at the venue. If it has no staff you will need to recruit at least three able-bodied assistants. This team will be working flat out to rig the lighting, as the time between shows in some theatres can often be quite minimal. In touring theatre you can find you have only a day to get in, rig and tech a whole production!

GETTING-IN AND FITTING-UP

A "get-in" is the term used for the process of getting the production, scenery, lights and performers into the theatre. Time has to be divided between all of these different aspects, and careful planning is necessary to ensure that everyone has enough time to do what needs to be done in the acting area. The theatre will be in great demand from the set designers and actors, who will need to use the space as well as you. This all adds to the general air of panic. So it is a great advantage to plan as far ahead as possible. Remember you need, and have a right to, time in the theatre, so stand your ground, in the nicest possible way of course!

Always use a safety chain after clamping the lantern in place.

SAFETY

Theatres can be very dangerous places, so it is vitally important to follow safe working methods. Electricity can kill, as can falling lanterns and other equipment, and there is the ever-present danger of fire. All theatres are subject to local fire and safety regulations which cover details like how close you can place lanterns to the audience and the actors, which substances are prohibited on a stage, exit lighting, and so on.

Common sense demands that you always work with the power off, and check that all electrical equipment is properly connected and earthed. Overhaul all lanterns and cables once a season. Cables should also be taped down. Hard hats and safety harnesses should be worn at all times. It is inevitable that at some time someone will accidentally drop something, so you should be aware of this danger. The cry of "heads" is usual to warn people that something is falling. Don't leave objects on top of ladders. Wear protective gloves when handling hot lanterns, gel holders, gobos and so on.

Safety chains and clamps are used to attach lanterns to the lighting bars; don't use any other form of attachment. Tighten the clamp first, then add a safety chain to secure the lantern should the clamp fail in any way. When lifting lanterns make sure that everything on the lantern is secure, so, for example, remove the gel holders. If you are using a rope to haul lanterns, be careful that it does not get worn by rubbing over abrasive surfaces, and that it is strong enough to take the weight. Don't just attach the rope to the clamp as this may not be secure. Run it through the yoke of the lantern first.

Ladders should always be braced by another member of the lighting team to prevent slipping.

This can be a tedious process but it may save a life or two! Check that the ladder is not damaged. If you use an A-frame ladder, ensure that it is fully extended and locked. Always be aware of how near the edge of the stage you are, and never lean out from the ladder; get off and move it. If you use a lighting tower or tallescope, you need another member of the team to move it and lock it in position.

If you have to take down another rig before setting your own, begin by unplugging all the cables from the dimmers, then unplug them from the lighting bar and coil and tape them. Next remove all the gel frames, gobos and so on from the lanterns and close any barn doors to prevent damage. Remember before removing any lanterns to check if the lighting bar is counter-weighted. If it is, you must remove the weights first, or you might as well take up flying as a hobby.

NEVER lift heavy weights unaided. A back injury can stay with you for life and ruin your career. If you do have to lift anything heavy, keep your back straight and bend your legs. Displays of machismo are foolish and to be avoided.

Fire-fighting and first-aid equipment must always be on hand. Be careful not to obscure

any danger or exit signs or fire regulation points. Be thorough in your checking of the theatre. Make sure you know its power capacity, which sockets are to be used for which lanterns, and where the different phases run in the building.

PRODUCTION SCHEDULE

PREPARATION: WEEKS 9–7

Lighting		Get plan of set and lighting plan of theatre. Check your stock. Prepare budget and draw up personnel needs.
Director		Cast list. Prepare rehearsal schedules.
Production manager		Continue to oversee production and budget.
Stage management		Gather rehearsal props. Find rehearsal space. Prepare prompt copy of script.
Sound		Agree rehearsal schedules.
Music		Agree rehearsal schedules. Gather musicians.
Choreography		Agree rehearsal schedules.

Use dry powder or CO_2 for electrical fires.

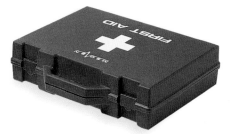
First-aid equipment should be regularly maintained and always to hand.

RIGGING

This is the term used to describe the hanging of the lanterns. If there is a previous rig in place, you may need to remove all or part of it, but it might save time to check and see if it is possible to incorporate some of the elements into your own design.

The lanterns are fitted on to lighting bars, lighting stands or booms. Lighting bars can be counter-weighted, winched or permanently fixed in position. They may be wired internally as a permanent arrangement or they may need to be cabled. A fixed network of these bars makes up the lighting grid.

Lighting stands or tripods can also be used to support lanterns, either on spigots or by G-clamps from a T-bar. A boom is a vertical lighting bar to which boom arms

can be attached. Boom arms can also be attached to walls or parts of the set.

When it comes to hanging the lanterns, you should be aware of the safety aspects and make sure all ladders or tallescopes are properly attended and supported. Then follow the correct order of hanging:
• Hang the lantern in place, lock the clamp, then secure the safety chain.
• Point the lantern in roughly the right direction.
• Put the colour in.
• Plug the lantern into the appropriate socket.

Cabling is often required even with ready-wired lighting bars. Start at the opposite end of the bar to its finishing point. Ensure that the cable you are using is long enough, as connections can

A neat, well-spaced rig.

be awkward and make fault-finding very difficult. If you are using extension cable, tie the socket of the cable around the bar next to the lantern and tape it along the bar at intervals. Label everything and mark each plug top with the socket number shown on the plan, and check this against the lighting plan. It is important to check the phasing at this point and make sure you are not bringing one phase into contact with another.

Each lantern and cable is plugged into a marked socket. These sockets may run straight back to the dimmers or through a

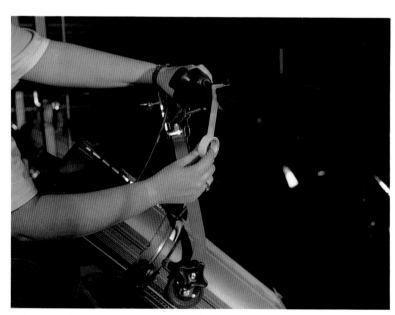

Tape loose cables neatly. Remember to leave enough slack so that you can focus the lantern properly.

Always keep plenty of gaffer tape to hand – it will help you produce a tidy rig.

PRODUCTION SCHEDULE

Lighting Production meeting. Contact stage manager/director/designer.

Director Production meeting. Work on script, e.g. cutting and running time.

Administration Programme material. Begin publicity displays.

Production manager Production meeting. Budgeting.

Stage management Prepare rehearsal space. Production meetings.

Set design Planning and technical meetings. Attend initial rehearsal.

Costume design First rehearsal.

Sound Production meeting and provisional sound tapes.

Music Singing and music rehearsals.

Choreography Dance and fight rehearsals.

Lighting Liaison with designers and director.

Director Rehearsals (sometimes blocking).

Administration Press and publicity.

Production manager Coordination of all technical aspects and budget.

Stage management Liaison with all departments. Running rehearsals. Making and finding props.

Set design Construction and liaison with stage manager.

Costume design Artwork.

Sound Liaison with director. Gather effects, etc.

Music As above.

Choreography As above.

patching system, where they terminate as plugs. Those to be used are then plugged into sockets which in turn run to the dimmers, and so to the lighting control board.

FOCUSING

This is perhaps the most important part of the production procedure. A focusing team needs four or five people: the lighting designer, on the floor giving instructions; the control-board operator, fading the lanterns in and out; the electrician, on top of the ladder focusing each lantern; and one or two people to steady the ladder or move the tower, and to run errands.

The control-board operator fades the lantern to be focused up before fading the previous one down, to prevent the stage being plunged into a dangerous darkness. The lanterns are usually focused at about 90 per cent power as they have a tendency to blow if jiggled at a higher power. Any violent movement is likely to cause a bulb to blow.

Focus the lantern on a low intensity so that the filament is visible and you can see its centre, which you use to pinpoint the exact place to which you want the lantern to point. Remember to make sure that the focused position of the lantern will cover the actor completely, no matter whether he or she is standing, sitting or doing anything else. Turn up the lantern to its full intensity and

This lighting control-board operator is communicating with the other members of the focusing team via a headset intercom system – it saves shouting!

note the overall effect. The most effective place for the lighting designer during this process is on stage with the lantern focused behind them. They can then shout or signal instructions to the lantern focuser. Unfortunately, you will frequently find yourself doing the focusing, which involves a great deal of climbing up and down ladders!

Work as accurately as possible. This is a crucial time for

the lighting designer. You will need to check that all the lanterns in your design are fulfilling their function properly. Make sure they are covering enough of the designated area, and that they will not cause distracting shadows or be too obtrusive on the set. There are hundreds of things to be aware of, and you may have to revise your plan. If so, do it now; there may not be enough time later.

PRODUCTION SCHEDULE

Tallescopes can be used to reach awkward lighting positions. Safety outriggers must be fitted to them.

DEVELOPMENT: WEEK 4

Lighting	Check stock.
Director	Rehearsals. Liaison with sound and lighting.
Administration	Recruit front-of-house staff. Press and publicity.
Production manager	As above.
Stage management	As above.
Set design	Scenery painting and furniture acquisition.
Costume design	Fittings.
Sound	Liaison with director. Prepare effects tapes.
Music	As above.
Choreography	As above.

DEVELOPMENT: WEEK 3

Lighting	Rehearsal and run-through.
Director	Run-through. Music and dancing introduced.
Administration	Selling.
Production manager	Hire equipment. Contact venue.
Stage management	Sound and lighting meetings with director.
Set design	Continue scenery construction.
Costume design	Making and gathering costumes.
Sound	Special effects and recordings with actors. Hire equipment and design sound rig.
Music	Singers join rehearsals. Music rehearsals continue.
Choreography	Fights choreographed. Dancers join main rehearsals.

The Final Sessions

Once all the lanterns are focused and gelled, the lighting designer calls a lighting session, at which all the lighting cues are created and plotted on the control board. It is an opportunity to show the director and the set designer your vision, and for either of them to make final changes in your design and ensure that everyone is happy with the result.

The designer usually sits in the middle of the auditorium. Sometimes he or she has the lighting board and an operator; at others he or she is in contact with the operator. They have a copy of the script and the lighting plan, plus a small light to read by. As each cue is brought up, the deputy stage manager enters it on a master copy of the text. The cues are set up on the control board as instructed by the designer, then run through one by one according to the cue synopsis and either recorded on the computer memory or noted on a cue sheet. They are usually drawn up in systematic form and show the number of the cue (from your cue synopsis), the memory number for a computer-operated board or each circuit's individual level, the action on the board (e.g. fade, cross-fade, etc) and the time for the action and details of the next preset.

As you progress through the production cue by cue, you will be able to see how your design stands up. You will also receive guidance and suggestions from the rest of the production crew.

To this end it is a good idea only to put the lanterns up to about 60–70 per cent so you have some power in reserve, in case someone wants more light. You will also need a "walker", a person who walks about the stage to show how the lighting will strike the actors.

At the lighting session, the designer sits in the auditorium, often with the lighting board and the operator.

PRODUCTION SCHEDULE

You will need a "walker" to check that all the areas you think you are lighting in cue are actually lit.

DEVELOPMENT: WEEK 2

Lighting Finalize lighting design.

Director Rehearsal. Lighting and sound meetings.

Administration Press and photo call.

Production manager Arrange production week and get-ins and fit-ups.

Stage management Props lists and cue sheets plus liaison with lighting and sound.

Set design Liaison with lighting and sound. Check all props.

Costume design Fittings.

Sound Finish tapes and integrate sound into rehearsals.

Music Musicians in rehearsals. Music rehearsals continue.

Choreography Fights in rehearsal.

PRODUCTION WEEK: DAY 7

Lighting Hire equipment arrives. Preliminary rigging.

Director Rehearsals with props and available set.

Administration Front-of-house staff and box office.

Production manager Supervise, get in and set up.

Stage management Cue sheets, rehearsals and coordinating run-throughs.

Set design Fit-up.

Costume design Costumes ready.

Sound Hire equipment arrives. Sound checks with musicians.

Music Rehearsal.

Choreography Rehearsal.

After this you should be able to iron out most of the problems, to fine-tune your design to everyone's satisfaction and to note all of your cues. You will then be ready for the technical rehearsal and the final adjustments before zero hour – the first performance.

THE TECHNICAL REHEARSAL (TECH)

This is to test out and rehearse all the technical aspects of the production and, with luck, sort out any remaining problems. The deputy stage manager cues the switchboard operator, and the lighting states are fitted in with the rest of the production, including actors, sound, scene changes and so on. The lighting designer can stop the rehearsal if any problems arise. As this rehearsal gives everybody the opportunity to sort out their technical difficulties, it can sometimes last a long time, and there will be time for you to re-plot if necessary. Be patient, for it is an invaluable event.

The technical rehearsal can often take a long time to complete, but is worth every minute as it gives you the opportunity to check your design thoroughly.

THE DRESS REHEARSAL

This is a full try-out of the production with all the actors, the costumes, the full set and the lighting. With luck you may get more than one dress rehearsal. You should have time to get back on stage afterwards to make sure all the focusing is perfect, though this time must be negotiated with the stage manager, who may have a number of such requests to juggle with.

The dress rehearsal is the first time when you will see everything coming together. There are bound to be some problems to sort out even at this stage, so don't worry if things go a little wrong.

PRODUCTION SCHEDULE

DURING THE RUN

If you are not operating the lighting yourself, you should keep an eye on the production to make sure that everything is up to scratch. If you are operating it, you will need to maintain the rig. You may be touring with the production, in which case your life will be taken up with get-ins, get-outs, rigging, techs and so on. You will also have to troubleshoot, as a number of things can go wrong during production. However, with careful planning and maintenance, you should be able to avoid most serious problems and have a successful production.

Lighting designers may not take a bow, but they are as much a part of the art of theatre as the rest of the company.

PRODUCTION WEEK: DAY 6

Lighting	Rig.
Director	Rehearsals.
Administration	Programmes and front-of-house staff.
Production manager	Fit-up.
Stage management	Help with everything!
Set design	Fit-up.
Costume design	Distribute costumes.
Sound	Sound rig.
Music	Rehearsal.
Choreography	Rehearsal.

PRODUCTION WEEK: DAY 5

Lighting	Focusing.
Director	Run-through.
Production manager	Fit-up.
Stage management	Prepare move from rehearsal rooms to set.
Set design	Finish painting and fit-up.
Costume design	Attend run-through.
Sound	Attend run-through.
Music	Rehearsal, full orchestra and cast.
Choreography	Rehearsal.

PRODUCTION WEEK: DAY 4

Lighting	Lighting session for plotting.
Director	Lighting and sound plotting.
Production manager	Lighting and sound plotting.
Stage management	Dress set. Lighting and sound plotting.
Set design	Lighting and sound plotting.
Costume design	Run-through. Make-up.
Sound	Lighting and sound plotting.
Music	Rehearsal.
Choreography	Rehearsal.

Troubleshooting

TOO FEW LANTERNS

If you only have a small number of lanterns, first split the stage into the largest possible areas that the spread of the lanterns will cover. As long as you adhere to the rule that lanterns should be positioned at roughly 45 degrees from the horizontal and the vertical, you should be able to avoid hard shadows.

By placing three or four lanterns on the front-of-house bar to cover the downstage area, and then two more behind the proscenium arch or slightly off stage to light the upstage area, you should be able to produce a serviceable general cover.

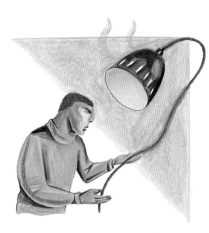

LANTERNS NOT WORKING OR SMOKING

Check the bulb to see if it has blown; check that the lantern has been called up on the switchboard; check the fuses, the patching and that the power to the dimmers is on. Also check the cable and finally, the internal wiring of the lantern. If it is smoking, switch it off! But remember that some gel colours and new gobos will smoke when first used.

GELS OR GOBOS BURNING OUT

This will happen anyway at some point. However, you should check the alignment of the bulb to make sure it is correct and not focusing too much light on the gel or gobo.

WEAK OUTPUT FROM A LANTERN

Check the switchboard, that is, look to see that the dimmer or master dimmer is in the correct position. Then re-check it by using another lantern, then by re-plugging the lantern into another circuit. Finally, check the bulb alignment.

FUSES BLOWING

Fuses blow in order to keep you safe. Don't try to replace a blown fuse with a larger one, or ignore it. Check through the whole rig for shorts if this keeps happening, and if in doubt call in an expert. Blown fuses can indicate a dangerous situation.

CONTROL BOARD MALFUNCTIONS

Always keep a back-up record of the lighting plots and cues. Although some computer memory boards do respond to being re-set, tampering with them is not a good idea. With manual boards, you should check the wiring and connections and that all the dimmers are receiving power. You should also check to see if anyone has used the board and tampered with your plotting information, or left anything on that shouldn't be on. If in doubt, ring the manufacturers and call in an expert.

WRONG COLOUR GEL

Go to another manufacturer. Also remember that you can mix gels to produce other colours.

DIFFERENT OUTPUT FROM PAIRED LANTERNS

Use a colour correction gel.

PRODUCTION SCHEDULE

ACTORS PERSIST IN MISSING THEIR "SPECIALS"

Reason with them, then place a small mark or a piece of luminous tape on the stage floor where you want them to stand.

Gobos will always burn out at some point, but it is worth checking that the bulb is aligned properly.

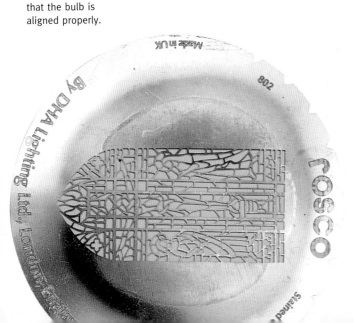

PRODUCTION WEEK: DAY 3

Lighting	Technical rehearsal.
Director	Tech.
Production manager	Tech.
Stage management	Rehearsal and tech.
Set design	Tech.
Costume design	Tech.
Sound	Tech.
Music	Tech and piano rehearsal.
Choreography	Rehearsal.

PRODUCTION WEEK: DAY 2

Lighting	Dress rehearsal. Notes and re-focusing.
Director	Dress rehearsal and notes. Photo call.
Administration	Photo call.
Production manager	Dress rehearsal.
Stage management	Run dress rehearsal. Attend notes session.
Set design	Photo call and dress rehearsal.
Sound	Dress rehearsal and notes.
Music	Dress rehearsal and notes.
Choreography	Dress rehearsal.

PRODUCTION WEEK: DAY 1

Lighting	Final dress and tech on stage.
Director	Final dress and notes.
Production manager	Final dress and tech on stage.
Stage management	Final dress and notes.
Set design	Final dress and last-minute work.
Sound	Final dress and notes.

Lighting Directory

This easy reference chart is provided to help the lighting designer identify the equipment available, and to give some basic information about it. The relevant sections in the chapter "Achieving the Effects" provide a more detailed description of the equipment and its uses.

Lamps (bulbs)

Type of bulb	Lantern	Features and characteristics
Linear	Floodlight	Incandescent tungsten-halogen bulb; handle with a dry cloth or gloves
Quartz-halogen	Profile, follow, fresnel and pebble-convex	As above
Glass	As above, and older floodlights	Low colour temperature; increasingly obsolete
Par	Parcan	Sealed unit containing bulb, lens and reflector
Discharge	Follow spots and fresnels	Economical to run but difficult to dim; used mainly in TV and film

Dimmer Racks

Control Boards

Manual

Computerized

Computerized with console

Lanterns

Lantern	Symbol	Type of beam	Focusing	Irises, shutters, gates and barn doors	Picture
Profile and ellipsoid spots Prelude Minuette zoom Silhouette Cantata Eurospot Acclaim zoomspot Flower spot		Hard-edged beam of fixed size with minimum flare; beam can be adjusted by field adjuster, usually underneath the lantern/	Hard or soft focusing achieved by moving lens	Iris allows beam size to be changed while shutters alter its shape	
Follow spot		Same as profile and ellipsoid	Same as profile and ellipsoid	Irises and shutters to shape beam	
Fresnel spot Quartet Starlette		Soft-edged and ill-defined beam	Soft focus only; lamp and reflector are moved towards or away from lens	Barn doors fitted to the front of the lantern allow the beam to be shaped	
Pebble-convex		Similar to profile with no flare outside the beam	As for fresnel	Barn doors shape beam	
Parcan		Very bright, narrow oval beam; there are several fixed beam widths	Cannot be focused	None	
Floods and cyc floods Strip lights		Wide spread beam	No focus	None	
Beam light		Similar to parcan but not as bright	Beam can be focused as for profile and ellipsoid	None	
Special effects lanterns Effects projector Colour changers Flicker wheels Colour scroller Animation disc Gobo		Depends on required effect; can be as for profile or fresnel	As before	As before	

Glossary

Adapter
A device which allows two or more electrical appliances to share the same power point.

Ampère (amps)
The unit of measurement of current flow in an electrical circuit.

Apron
Extension of the stage beyond the proscenium arch.

Auditorium
The area of the theatre where the audience sits during a performance.

Backcloth
A cloth, often painted, suspended across the back of the stage.

Bar
A rod or pipe suspended above the stage from which lanterns, scenery and so on can be hung.

Barn doors
Four hinged shutters which can be fitted to the front of a lantern to shape the beam of light.

Batten
1. A rod or pipe suspended above the stage from which lanterns, scenery, etc, can be hung (see Bar)
2. A piece of wood used to connect two flats.

3. Lanterns suspended over the stage or used as border lights.
4. A piece of wood used to keep a suspended cloth taut and straight.

Beam light
A lantern which has no lens and gives a straight beam of light.

Bifocal spot
A spotlight which, through the addition of extra shutters, can produce a hard- or soft-edged beam.

Black light
Ultra-violet light.

Blanket colour
A wash of colour of the same tint over a large area.

Blocking
The arrangement and setting of the actors' moves on the stage.

Boom
A vertical lighting bar.

Boom arm
A device used to hang a lantern from a boom.

Border
A flat or curtain suspended so as to conceal the lighting and stage machinery above the stage from the audience.

Box set
A set which encloses the acting area on three sides, often a room with the fourth wall removed.

Brace
A support used to secure flats.

Bridge
A walkway above the stage used to reach stage equipment.

Centreline
An imaginary line down the centre of the stage from front to back.

Channel
A circuit in the lighting system.

Chase
A sequence of lighting states which change in a repeatable pattern.

Check
Lower the intensity of light.

Circuit
The connection from the lantern to the dimmer or patching panel.

Clamp
Used to fasten lanterns to lighting bars; it may come in a C or G form.

Colour call
The colour gels required for a lighting design.

Colour frame
The frame which holds the colour filter in front of a lantern.

Colour medium
A translucent colour filter placed in front of a lantern to colour the light.

Colour wheel
A wheel containing a number of colour mediums which is mounted on the front of a lantern and can be rotated to change the colour of the light emitted by the lantern.

Control board
Panel used to control the lighting.

Counterweights
Weights used to balance flying bars loaded with scenery or lights, so they can be raised or lowered.

Crossfade
A way of moving from one lighting state to another without dimming to darkness.

Cue
1. A physical action in a performance which tells a performer when to enter, speak a line, etc.
2. The point in a production which indicates a change of lighting state. This can be a line, a movement or a song, as long as it is recognizable by the board operator.

Cue light
A box with two lights which tells when a cue is due (red) and when to go (green) on the cue.

Cue sheet
A sheet used by the board operator on which all the lighting cues and states in a production are recorded.

Cue-to-cue
A rehearsal which jumps from one cue to the next in order to check the effects.

Cyclorama
A backcloth hung at the rear of the stage and usually lit.

De-rig
To remove a lighting rig at the end of a production.

Dim
To decrease the intensity of light.

Dimmer
The apparatus which dims the lanterns.

Dip
A covered hole on the stage which houses electrical sockets.

Dock
An area for storing scenery when not in use.

Downstage
The area of stage nearest the audience; the front of the stage.

Dress circle
The area of seating in the auditorium above the orchestra.

Dress rehearsal
A full try-out of the production just prior to opening, using full costume and effects.

Dry ice
A form of frozen carbon dioxide used to produce mist effects.

Earthing
The wiring of the metal parts of electrical equipment to the ground.

Ellipsoidal
A type of reflector used in profile spots.

Fader
Switch on control board used to vary the output of a lantern.

Fill light
Used to fill in the shadows created by a key light.

Fit-up
The rigging of lights, sound, scenery, etc, in a theatre prior to the opening of a production.

Glossary

Flare
The spill from a lantern.

Flat
A screen made of a sheet of wood or cloth that is attached to a wooden frame.

Flies
The area directly above the stage in which scenery, lighting and other equipment can be kept.

Floodlights
Lanterns which give a wide beam of light.

Floorcloth
A canvas sheet, usually painted, placed on the floor of the stage as part of the stage design.

Flown
Describing something which is suspended above the stage, which can also be made to appear or disappear in front of an audience and so become a flown element in the overall production.

Fly
To bring scenery or equipment in or out of the stage area vertically.

Fly floor
The platform from which the flies are operated.

Focusing
Arranging the position, direction, cover and shape of the beam of light from a lantern.

Follow spot
A lantern directed at an actor which follows his or her movements around the stage.

Footlights or floats
A batten of lights set at the front of the stage on the floor.

Fourth wall
The invisible "wall" which stands between the audience and the stage in a box set. The term is sometimes used to refer to the barrier between the audience and the stage action.

Fresnel
A spotlight with a lens which gives an even field of light with a soft-edged beam.

Front-of-house lights
Lighting suspended in the auditorium and directed towards the stage.

Gaffer tape
A cloth-backed tape with adhesive on one side which is tearable but strong and is generally easily removed. It is used to tape cables and practically anything else. It is an invaluable asset in rigging and making safe. It usually comes in large rolls and a number of different colours, black being most useful as it does not show up in general lighting.

Gate
An aperture on a profile spot between the light source and the lens. The beam from the lantern may be shaped by placing shutters, an iris or a gobo in here.

Gauze
See Scrim.

Gel
A colour filter medium used to alter the colour of the beam of light from a lantern.

Get-in/Get-out
The process of taking a production into or out of a theatre.

Gobo
A thin metal plate with a cut-out design which when inserted into (usually) a profile spot causes an image of the design to be projected on to the stage.

Grid
A metal frame from which equipment is suspended.

Ground plan
A scale drawing of the set viewed from above.

Ground-row lighting
A strip of lanterns placed on the floor for low-level lighting effects or to light scenery from below.

Half
A warning call given to the company 35 minutes before the start of the show.

Hand prop
A prop handled by an actor.

Hanging
Attaching pieces of equipment or scenery to bars.

Hook clamp
A clamp which holds a lantern or lantern onto a lighting bar.

House
The audience or, in opera, the entire theatre, including the performing company.

Inset
A small scene which is set inside a larger scene.

Iris
A device inserted into a lantern to vary the size of the beam.

Iron
A curtain lowered downstage of the tabs in case of fire.

Key light
The most dominant direction of the lighting which is of greatest importance on the set.

Ladder
A ladder-shaped frame for hanging lanterns on, usually as side lights. This cannot be climbed.

Lamp
The electric light bulb that is used in a lantern.

Lantern
See Luminaire.

Leg
A cloth, hung vertically from the flies and used to mask the sides of the stage.

Levels
Indicator of the intensity of light.

Lighting bar
A batten or pipe used to attach lighting equipment to.

Lighting plan
A scale drawing showing the location of each lantern or other piece of equipment.

Lighting session
A rehearsal of lighting effects on stage during which adjustments to the lanterns can be made.

Lighting state
The structure of the lighting used at a particular time.

Limes
Jargon for a follow spot.

Luminaire
A piece of lighting equipment which holds the lamp and is used to project the light.

Magazine battens
Battens of lights which are flown above the stage.

Marking
Either deployment of a substitute for a real prop or piece of scenery during rehearsals, or not playing a role to its full power during rehearsal to save energy, voice, etc.

Mark out
A system of lines marked or taped onto the floor of the rehearsal room to designate the layout of the stage.

Maroon
A pyrotechnic device which produces a loud explosion.

Glossary

Masking
Hiding parts of the stage or equipment from the audience. Also when one actor obscures another.

Master (grand master)
A dimmer control which controls the submasters.

Memory board
A lighting control system which stores lighting levels electronically.

Mock-up
A model of the stage or set used as a forerunner to the final model.

Offstage
Any backstage area that cannot be seen by the audience.

Orchestra
The ground-floor seats in a theatre.

Pairing
Joining more than one lantern to one circuit.

Pan
1. Movement of lighting from side to side.
2. Water-based stage make-up, short for pancake.

Panorama
A painted cloth wound across the stage to show a changing view.

Parcan
A lantern holding a par lamp (a single unit lens and reflector).

Patching
The use of a cross-connecting panel which allows any of the stage circuits to be connected to any dimmer.

Perch
A lighting position concealed behind the proscenium arch.

Plot
1. The action of a play.
2. A list of cues or effects used in a production.

Practical
Any onstage working apparatus, such as a light switch or water tap.

Preset
1. Basic lighting state seen by the audience before the performance commences.
2. A prop or object placed before the performance commences.

Projector
Floodlight.

Prompt copy
Copy of the script from which the show is run, containing all of the production details.

Prompt corner
Desk and console at the side of the stage from which the stage manager runs the show.

Props (properties)
Any item apart from costume or scenery used by the actors during the performance.

Proscenium arch
The arch which stands between the stage and the auditorium in most conventional theatres.

Pyrotechnics
Bangs and flashes!

Quarter
Backstage call, 15 minutes before beginners (first performers on stage taking their places) and 20 minutes before curtain-up.

Read through
A reading of the play without any of the action.

Reflector
The shiny, reflective surface at the back of a lantern which intensifies the beam.

Rig
The arrangement of all the items of lighting equipment for a particular theatrical production.

Rigging
Fixing of lanterns into the appropriate places. This generally takes place in the last week of the production period.

Run
1. The number of performances of a work.
2. A run through of a work.

Runners
A pair of curtains which part at the centre.

Scatter
Light falling outside of the main beam of a spot.

Scrim
A cloth made of an open-weave material which can be painted. It becomes opaque when lit from the front and transparent when lit from behind. A combination of lighting angles can make it translucent, so that the cloth is semi-visible as well as whatever is behind it.

Shutter
A device on the front of a lantern which can alter the shape of the beam of light.

Sight line
The angles of visibility from the audience point of view.

Special
A piece of lighting equipment which performs a particular effect but is not used for general lighting of the stage area.

Spill
Unwanted light onstage.

Spot (spotlight)
A lantern producing a small circle of light which can be controlled by focusing.

Stage cloth
A piece of painted canvas that is hung vertically.

Stagger
A run through of a work aimed at getting the flow of the piece.

Stalls
See Orchestra.

Tabs
Curtains, usually across the front of the stage.

Tallescope
A mobile scaffolding tower which is used to hang equipment and lanterns from high bars.

Throw
The distance between the lantern and the area lit.

Thrust stage
A stage which projects into the auditorium area.

Trap
A hole in the stage which allows access from below.

Trapeze
Single-hang lighting bar.

Upstage
The area of stage furthest from the front of the stage.

Volt
A unit of measurement of the electrical pressure between two points in a circuit.

Walk through
A rehearsal where the cast will go through all of the moves, entrances and exits in a production.

Ways
The maximum number of combinations of channels in a lighting installation.

Wings
The areas at the side of the stage concealed from the audience.

Workshop
An area backstage which is non-performing.

Index

Index

Credits

Quarto would like to acknowledge and thank the following for providing pictures used in this book. While every effort has been made to acknowledge copyright holders, we would like to apologize should there have been any omissions.

Key: **t** top **b** below **r** right **l** left **c** centre

Ace Photo Agency 15cr, 129b; Altman Stage Lighting Co. Inc. 53b; CCT Lighting 67, 132bc; bulbs supplied by GE Lighting Ltd 48, 49, 50, 51, 132a; Instant Zipup Ltd 125; Joel Finler Collection 38b; Le Maitre 111b, 114b, 115b; Effects projector supplied by Optikinetics Ltd 100bl; The Panic Pictures Library 7, 9br, 15tl, 30, 31, 42, 43t&b, 79t&b, 81t, 88, 94b, 102, 103b, 104t&b, 106b, 108b, 113t&b, 115t, 126, 128b; Strand Lighting Ltd 5tl&tr, 58t, 59t, 62t, 64t, 133 3rd down; The Mansell Collection 8, 9bl; Teatro (UK) Ltd 1, 52, 56t, 62b, 63t, 65t, 98t, 99b, 109t&b, 133 1st, 2nd, 4th, 5th & 6th down; Visual Arts Library 80

The following kindly loaned items for use in photography.

GE Lighting Ltd
Melton Road
Leicester LE4 7PD

Dancia International
187 Drury Lane
London WC2

Paul Forrester
151 City Road
London EC1 1JH

Optikinetics Ltd
38 Cromwell Road
Luton LU3 1DN

Pleasance Theatre
North Road
London N7 9EF

Quarto would like to thank the following people at the Pleasance Theatre for their help and expertise during the production of this book.

Amanda Castille, Stage Manager, who created all of the lighting effects which were photographed at the Pleasance specifically for use in this book.

Dan Watkins, Consultant for Theatre Futures, who kindly gave advice on many of the illustrations featured in the book, and also gave several helpful and informative tours around the Pleasance Theatre.

Anthony Alderson, who modelled onstage for several of the photographs used inside the book.

Christopher Richardson, Set Designer, who allowed us to photograph his set for the play *From Morning Sun 'til Dusk*, written and directed by **Angus Graham-Campbell**, lighting director **Dan Watkins**.

We would also like to acknowledge and thank the following people.

Philip Shaw, who provided artwork reference and checked the illustrations featured in the book (including examples of lighting designs and lantern cross-sections), and also helped to write many of the accompanying captions.

Chris Pearce, of The Panic Pictures Library, who helped during the selection of production stills.

Student actor **Theodore Jansen**, who modelled for the jacket photographs.